English for Business

KEY BUSINESS SKILLS

Barry Tomalin

Collins

HarperCollins Publishers
77-85 Fulham Palace Road
London W6 8JB

First edition 2012

Reprint 10 9 8 7 6 5 4 3 2 1 0

© HarperCollins Publishers 2012

ISBN 978-0-00-748879-7

Collins® is a registered trademark of HarperCollins
Publishers Limited.

www.collinselt.com

A catalogue record for this book is available from
the British Library.

Typeset in India by Aptara.

Printed and bound in Italy by LEGO SpA,
Lavis (Trento).

About the author

Barry Tomalin is Director of Cultural Training at International House in London and Visiting Lecturer in Cultural Awareness and International Communication at the London Academy of Diplomacy, University of East Anglia. He is also a former producer and presenter in the BBC English department of the BBC World Service. Barry has worked in over 50 countries worldwide, designing and delivering training programmes for business and international organizations.

ACKNOWLEDGEMENTS

Thanks to Marlene Regaya, Lea Paolini and Maurice Cassidy of International House, and especially to Will Capel for turning a successful taught course into a self-study book.

Barry Tomalin

Contents

Introduction

Collins English for Business: Key Business Skills will help you communicate successfully either internationally company-to-company or within a multinational company.

You can use *Key Business Skills*:

- as a self-study course
- as a resource for business communication or business English courses

Key Business Skills focuses on four key communication skills areas:

- Networking
- Presentations
- Meetings
- Negotiations

Key Business Skills comprises a **book** and **CD**. The **book** has 12 units. At the back of the book there is:

- the Business file – additional reference material
- the Answer key
- the Audio scripts for the audio recordings

Unit structure

Each of the 12 units of *Key Business Skills* is divided into two parts.

Part A contains these sections:

- Aims – This sets out the objectives for both Parts A and B of the unit.
- Quiz – This raises self-awareness about the topic and introduces the communication skills focus for both Parts A and B of the unit.
- Briefing – This presents the communication skills for Part A.
- Listening – This gives you the opportunity to listen to a conversation, presentation, meeting or negotiation that shows you how to use the communication skills you have read about in the Briefing.
- Business practice – This presents the key language and provides speaking and vocabulary practice based on the communication skills.
- Business culture – This provides information on how the communication skills you have learned may differ in different international situations.

Part B contains these sections:

- Briefing – This presents the communication skills focus for Part B.
- Listening – This gives you the opportunity to listen to a conversation, presentation, meeting or negotiation that shows you how to use the communication skills you have read about in the Briefing.
- Business practice – This presents the key language and provides speaking and vocabulary practice based on the communication skills.
- Business writing – This provides presentation and practice of writing tasks associated with the unit topic.

- Key take-aways – This is a reflective section to help you record what you have learned and how you will use it in future.
- Business file – This section at the back of the book provides you with additional reference material for the Business culture and Business writing parts in some of the units.

Using the CD

This icon indicates that there is an audio track that you should listen to. The CD contains the MP3 files for the Listening and Business practice sections. Please note that the *Key Business Skills* CD is designed for use with a computer. If you want to play the audio on a CD player, you should download the tracks to your computer and then burn all the tracks onto an audio CD.

'Business Plus' approach

This book uses the 'Business Plus' approach that teaches you international business skills AND provides you with the language you need. An important part of this approach is the teaching and practice of the set phrases which international managers use all the time in international communication. The Business practice sections in the book contain these phrases together with audio support so that you can listen and repeat and become fluent at using these phrases.

Powered by COBUILD

Words or phrases in *Key Business Skills* that were felt too advanced for intermediate (B1) learners have been glossed using the definitions from the *Collins COBUILD Advanced Dictionary*.

Using *Key Business Skills*

You can either work through the units from Unit 1 to Unit 12 or you can choose the units and topics that are most useful to you. The Contents page will help in your selection of units for study.

Study tips

- Each unit takes about two hours – one hour per part. Take regular breaks and do not try to study for too long. Thirty minutes is a sensible study period.
- Regular study is better than occasional intensive study.
- Read the unit through first to get an overview without doing any exercises. This will help you see what you want to focus on.
- Put the audio tracks on your mobile phone or MP3 player so you can listen to the conversations as many times as you need to and do the activities on your way to work or when you are out and about.
- Try to find someone with whom you can practise your English, either face-to-face, over the phone or online using a webcam.
- Make sure you complete the Key take-aways section and refer to it regularly. It will remind you of what you have found useful, and how and when you intend to apply it.

Language level

Key Business Skills has been written for business learners at B1–C1 level of the Common European Framework of Reference for Languages (CEFR) (Intermediate to Advanced).

Other titles

Also available in the *Collins English for Business* series: *Listening*, *Speaking*, *Reading* and *Writing*.

1 Introductions

You never get a second chance to make a first impression.

Aims

- How to introduce yourself
- What to say and what to do
- Why introductions are important
- PAPO – How to describe your project
- International business card etiquette

A How to introduce yourself

Quiz

What information do you like or need to give when you introduce yourself? Tick the boxes.

1	name	
2	address	
3	nationality	
4	qualifications	
5	job title	
6	company	
7	responsibilities	
8	company location	
9	purpose of visit	
10	family information	

The elevator pitch

Imagine you are in the elevator of an office you are visiting. You recognize that an important client who does not know you is standing there. You have a maximum of 30 seconds to introduce yourself and make an impression. Think about what you will say. Then read the Briefing.

Briefing

Making a good first impression is an important skill but most people don't do it very well. They get confused. They say the wrong thing. They forget the most important information.

So what do you need to say? Remember these six things.

1	Name	Say your name CLEARLY. Pause between your given (first) name and your family name.
2	Nationality	Say where you come from. This may help people identify your accent and make you easier to understand.
3	Job	Say your job. Give your job title or say what your job is.
4	Company	Give the company name. Say which company you work for.
5	Location	Give the location of the company.
6	Pitch	Make a *pitch*. Give a reason for talking to the person. Say why you are here. Describe in one sentence your responsibilities. A *pitch* is what you do to make the other person interested in you.

Be careful about:

- shaking hands – maybe wait until they offer you their hand.
- making jokes – people can take them seriously, misunderstand or be insulted.
- asking people to do something – they may not be able to help or they may not want to. Don't alienate people, encourage them.

Listening

1 Listen to seven people introducing themselves at an international conference. They did not include all the information about themselves. Put a tick if they gave the information. Which speaker gave all the necessary information?

	Name	Nationality	Job	Company	Location	Pitch
Speaker 1						
Speaker 2						
Speaker 3						
Speaker 4						
Speaker 5						
Speaker 6						
Speaker 7						

2 Listen again to the seven people and say if these statements are true or false.

1 Speaker 1 is a human resources manager.   True ☐   False ☐

2 Speaker 2 works for a petrol station company.   True ☐   False ☐

3 Speaker 3 is based in London.   True ☐   False ☐

4 Speaker 4 works in Edinburgh.   True ☐   False ☐

5 Speaker 5's company has its headquarters in Stuttgart.   True ☐   False ☐

6 Speaker 6 works in Europe.   True ☐   False ☐

7 Speaker 7 works in Kerala, India.   True ☐   False ☐

Business practice

1 Listen and repeat these sentences.

Say hello	Hi, I'm (*your name*).
	Hello, my name's (*your name*).
	Good morning / Good afternoon / Good evening, my name's …
	Can / May I introduce myself? My name's …
Say where you are from	I'm from Rio de Janeiro in Brazil.
	I'm Brazilian.
	I come from Rio.
Say what your job is	I'm a project manager and IT specialist.
	I work as an accountant for a big US corporation.
Say where you work	I work for / with Petrobras, the oil and gas company.
Give the company's location	The company is based in Rio de Janeiro.
	We're located in a suburb of Stuttgart.
Say why you are here and what you are doing	I'm responsible for overseas suppliers and I'm here to make an agreement with a new contractor.

2 Test yourself. Cover the sentences above and then complete these sentences.

1 I'm responsible .... sales in Eastern Europe.

2 .... I give you my card?

3 The company is .... in Switzerland.

4   I'm .... the USA.

5   I'm .... to network.

6   I'm .... for IT systems.

7   The company is .... in the city centre.

8   Hi, may I .... myself?

3   **Listen to this introduction and repeat it. Try to copy the intonation.**

> Hello. May I introduce myself? I'm Alex Johnson. I'm from Leeds in the UK. I'm a systems analyst in IBM, based in Leeds, and I'm currently working with a team here to evaluate our new telecoms application.

Now record your own introduction. Don't forget to make your *pitch*. Listen to it and compare. Did you sound clear, interesting and friendly? If you can, ask a colleague or friend to listen to it to give you their opinion.

Business culture

People in different parts of the world have different customs when exchanging business cards.

Study this table. What is the etiquette where you live and work?

Europe	Asia
Give the business card at any time.	Offer the card first when you meet.
Don't do a special presentation.	Offer it with both hands, card facing outwards.
Give it with one hand or leave it on the table.	Read it carefully and comment.
Put it in a pocket or notebook.	Put it in a card holder.
Write extra information on it if you need to.	Never write on it.

What's the difference? In Europe, and also in the Americas, the business card is simply a means of follow-up contact. In Asia it is a ritual and a record of your business network. If you treat the business card seriously, it means you are serious about the people you are meeting.

How to describe your current project

Briefing

It is important to be able to describe your current project – what you are working on right now. Use this formula to describe your job and your current project simply and clearly.

P	Project title	First, say what the name of your project is.
A	Project aim	Next, say what its aims are.
P	Project process	Then say how you are organizing you project.
O	Project outcome	Finally, say what the outcome or result will be.

If you do this well, your partner or client will be able to ask questions to get more information or to clarify anything that is necessary.

Listening

1 Here are four PAPO descriptions. Listen and write down the key information. Pause the audio and listen again when you need to.

Current project 1		Current project 2	
P		P	
A		A	
P		P	
O		O	

Current project 3		Current project 4	
P		P	
A		A	
P		P	
O		O	

2 **Listen again to the four PAPO descriptions.**

1 In Current project 1 what word or phrase tells you that the schedule for the report will be difficult to achieve?

2 In Current project 2 what word or phrase tells you there is an obligation to submit the bid by the end of the year?

3 In Current project 3 what word or phrase means *now*?

4 In Current project 4 what word or phrase means the same as *aim*?

Business practice

1 **Listen and repeat these sentences.**

P	How to describe your project title
	The focus of my current project is …
	The project I'm working on right now is …
	The project I'm currently responsible for is …
A	**How to describe your project aim**
	The aims and objectives of the project are …
	It's a project which is designed to …
	The project aims to …
P	**How to describe your project process**
	The project is organized in three stages: plan, build and run.
	There are three phases in the project: project research, materials design and project dissemination.
	The project is divided into three main areas: sourcing contractors, agreeing contracts and managing the supply chain.
O	**How to describe your project outcome**
	You can describe the project outcomes in terms of QUALITY or of TIME.
	QUALITY OUTCOMES
	The project outcomes will be increased customer support, reduced customer complaints and higher overall customer satisfaction.
	The outcome of the project will be improved performance and deeper staff engagement with the product and with the company.
	TIME OUTCOMES
	Stage one will be completed by December.
	The project is due for completion by this time next year.

Glossary

To **disseminate** information or knowledge means to distribute it so that it reaches many people or organizations.

2 **Test yourself. Complete the sentences with words from the box.**

based	outcome	responsible	purpose
agreement	contractor	supplier	overseas

1 I hope the .... of this negotiation will be successful.

2 If all goes well we expect to make an .... by next month.

3 I'm .... for the supply chain.

4 Tell me the .... of your visit.

5 I'm a .... to some of the largest companies in Britain.

6 My company is .... in Dusseldorf in Germany but I work in Delhi.

7 I'm here to find a .... to build the new power station.

8 My job is to manage .... operations.

3 **Test yourself. Complete the sentences with prepositions from the box.**

on	in	for

1 My company is based .... Thailand.

2 I'm responsible .... four hundred employees.

3 I work .... a large multinational.

4 I'm working .... a new project.

5 The project is organized .... three stages.

6 I am collaborating .... the project with three other companies.

4 **You are at a conference and a business partner asks you about your current project. Listen and answer his questions.**

Partner: Tell me what you're working on right now.

You: ....

Partner: Sounds interesting. What are its aims?

You: ....

Partner: I see. And tell me how you're running the project.

You: ....

Partner: And what will the outcome be? What are you hoping for?

You: ....

Partner: That's very interesting. Let me tell you what I'm working on at the moment. We're looking for a supplier who can …

Business writing

What's on your business card? Remember, you need more information for use internationally than you need in your own country. And you may need information in the language of your partners or clients.

Writing task

Study this business card and then design your own card.

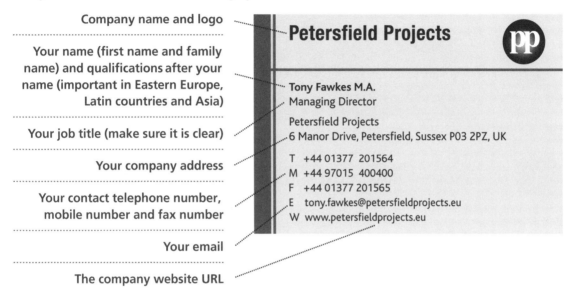

Company name and logo ....

Your name (first name and family name) and qualifications after your name (important in Eastern Europe, Latin countries and Asia) ....

Your job title (make sure it is clear) ....

Your company address ....

Your contact telephone number, mobile number and fax number ....

Your email ....

The company website URL ....

Petersfield Projects   **pp**

Tony Fawkes M.A.
Managing Director

Petersfield Projects
6 Manor Drive, Petersfield, Sussex PO3 2PZ, UK

T +44 01377 201564
M +44 97015 400400
F +44 01377 201565
E tony.fawkes@petersfieldprojects.eu
W www.petersfieldprojects.eu

Key take-aways

Write down the things you will take away from Unit 1 and how you will implement them.

Topic	Take-away	Implementation strategy – How?	Implementation time frame – When?
How to introduce yourself – the elevator pitch			
What you need to include in a personal introduction			
PAPO – How to describe your project			
What to put on your business card			
How to present your card in different parts of the world			

2 Listening

When he talks to you it is like no one else is in the room.
— Said about former US President Bill Clinton

Aims

- How to improve your listening skills with active listening
- How to build good relationships in conversation
- Use F.A.C.E. when speaking to people
- How to build good relationships when writing

A Active listening – the key to networking

Quiz

In business and social conversations what kind of listener are you?

In business and social conversations, what are you like? Tick the descriptions that match your style.

1	It is difficult for me to start a conversation with people I don't know.	
2	I like meeting new people. I go up to them and say hello.	
3	I prefer to spend time with people I know and like.	
4	I don't talk to people I don't know until someone introduces me.	
5	I often speak too much when I meet people.	
6	I interrupt people when they are talking to say what I want.	
7	I get impatient if I have to listen for too long.	
8	I judge what people say and if I don't like it I interrupt.	
9	I am happy to listen and not talk.	
10	I listen a lot. I don't interrupt and I pause before I reply.	

Now read the Briefing about the different types of listener that have been identified by research.

Briefing

The secret of successful networking and communication at work and in social situations is to be a good listener. Good talkers are first of all good listeners. Research has identified four types of listener:

- Non-listeners
- Marginal listeners
- Pretend listeners
- Active listeners

Non-listeners
Non-listeners are more interested in what they have to say themselves than in the person they are talking to. This means they monopolize the conversation and they talk all the time. They have a lot to say and they say it.

Marginal listeners
Marginal listeners are also more interested in what they have to say themselves than the person they are talking to. However, they use what the other person says as an introduction to what they want to say. They often interrupt so they can tell you what they are thinking. Marginal listeners often get impatient. They may show this by their eye movements, by tapping their fingers on the table or on their knee or by moving their feet a lot. They constantly check their mobile phones for text messages, emails and phone messages.

Pretend listeners
Pretend listeners appear to listen but they are observing your character and judging what you say. As they listen, they are deciding how to respond. Pretend listeners are concerned with what you say and how you say it. They are not concerned with how you feel. They 'hear the words' but they don't 'hear the feelings'.

Active listeners
Active listeners are quiet and sympathetic. They listen to what you say but they also pay attention to how you feel. You may be nervous or angry, or very happy and pleased. They encourage you to express what you want to say and to continue speaking. They don't interrupt. They wait for you to finish before they respond.

In reality we are probably all four types of listener at different times, depending on the conversation and how we feel! However, the more we can practise active listening the more people will want to listen to us. That is why people say the best listeners are often the best talkers.

Listening

1   **Listen to four conversations and decide what the listener's style is.**

Conversation	Style of listener
1 Paula	
2 Steve	
3 Kate	
4 Mr Klein	

07 **2** **Listen again to the four conversations and answer these questions.**

1   In Conversation 1 what does Paula say to show sympathy?

2   In Conversation 1 what does Paula say to show surprise?

3   In Conversation 2 how does Maria sound?

4   In Conversation 3 what does Kate say about Tom's good news?

5   In Conversation 4 what does Mr Klein do to interrupt the conversation?

Business practice

08 **1** **Listen and repeat these sentences. Remember that to show genuine interest in what the other person is saying, the way you say something can be as important as the words you use. Try to copy the intonation as closely as possible.**

Show interest	How are things?
	How's it going?
	Sounds interesting!
	How interesting!
	Really?
Show surprise	Really?
	Wow!
	No!
Show sympathy	Oh, dear!
	I'm sorry to hear that.
	Really!
	What a pity!
Show support	I'm sure we can fix this.
	I'm certain we can work this out.
	No problem. We'll deal with it.
	If you need any help, let me know.
Reassure	Don't worry about it.
	It'll be OK.
	Don't worry. Everything will be fine.
Praise or congratulate	Great!
	Well done!
	That's fantastic!
	Congratulations!

2 **Take part in this conversation and be an active listener. Listen to Nicky, a colleague, and respond, following the instructions. Then listen to the model conversation.**

Nicky: Hi there.

You: *Say hello. Ask about the project's progress.*

Nicky: Not very well, I'm afraid.

You: *Show sympathy.*

Nicky: Yes, we're over budget and late.

You: *Show surprise.*

Nicky: Yes, I'm a bit surprised too.

You: *Show support.*

Nicky: That would be great. Could I check my diary and fix a time for a meeting?

You: *Reassure.*

3 **Take part in a conversation with another colleague, Sam, and respond, following the instructions. Then listen to the model conversation.**

Sam: Hello.

You: *Say hello. Ask how things are.*

Sam: I wanted to ring and tell you. I got the promotion!

You: *Show surprise.*

Sam: Yes. I start next month.

You: *Congratulate Sam.*

Sam: Thanks. It's going to be hard work.

You: *Offer support.*

Sam: Thanks, I'll remember that.

Business culture

When you are with someone and listening to them, you normally look at them. However, in many countries to look at someone straight in the eye can be interpreted as threatening, challenging or to a senior person even insubordinate. Look at the questionnaire on page 104 and tick the descriptions that match your style.

Using F.A.C.E.

Briefing

Have you noticed that it is very difficult to sit in silence and look at someone who is talking to you, unless, of course, it is a lecture? You want to show empathy and interest.

In a conversation we can use F.A.C.E. to help empathize with the person we are listening to and show interest in what they are saying. F.A.C.E. stands for:

F	Focus	**Focus** means you focus on the speaker and no one and nothing else. You focus not just on the words they say but also on how they feel. You try and appreciate the total experience of the communication without judging what they are saying. Make a noise to show you are focusing and understanding, for example *Uh huh* or *Mmm*.
A	Acknowledge	**Acknowledge** means you recognize the person. You may do this by moving your head to show you are listening. Or you may adapt your facial expression to what they are saying. For example, be serious if they are describing something serious or smile if they are telling a funny story. Use short expressions like *I see* or *I understand* to show you are paying attention.
C	Clarify	**Clarify** means you ask simple questions to encourage the speaker. Questions like *What happened next?* or *How did you feel?* encourage the speaker to talk more.
E	Empathize	**Empathize** means saying something to show you appreciate the speaker's opinion or experience.

If you use F.A.C.E, people will respond to you more and it will be easier to build positive relations with them.

Listening

1 Listen to four business conversations. Focus on the listener. What is the listener doing in each conversation?

- Focusing
- Acknowledging
- Clarifying
- Empathizing

Conversation	
1	
2	
3	
4	

2 **Listen again to the four conversations and answer these questions.**

1   In Conversation 1 what does the listener do to keep the conversation going?

2   In Conversation 2 does the listener sound excited or bored?

3   In Conversation 3 what does the listener say?

4   In Conversation 4 what expressions does the listener use to show she understands?

Business practice

1 **Listen and repeat these phrases. You saw some of them in 2A.**

F	Focus
	You do this with non-linguistic gestures, for example by looking the person in the eye or by holding your chin with your hand, and by using non-verbal language like Uh huh and Mmm. Uh huh. Mmm.
A	**Acknowledge**
	I see. (*to show you understand*) I'm with you. (*to show you understand*) Yes, of course. (*to show you agree*) That's true. (*to show you agree*) Really? (*to show surprise and interest*) Right! (*to show you understand and agree*) That's interesting.
C	**Clarify**
	What happened next? What did you do next? Could you say that again, please? Tell me a little bit more about that. Could you explain that in a bit more detail?
E	**Empathize**
	Great! How wonderful! (*if the other person is describing a success*) How awful! (*if it's bad*) Well done! (*to congratulate*) That's terrific! (*to celebrate good news*) That's really interesting. (*to show strong interest*)

🎧 **2** Use F.A.C.E. in this conversation to show you are listening well. Listen to Tim, a colleague, and respond, following the instructions. Then listen to the model conversation.

Tim: Have you heard the good news?

You: *Say no and ask for more information.*

Tim: We got the Canada contract.

You: *Acknowledge and congratulate Tim. And ask for more information.*

Tim: Well, we got an email confirming the deal last night.

You: *Clarify.*

Tim: The email was from the government.

You: *Say well done again.*

Tim: Thanks. We must find a way to celebrate.

You: *Agree.*

Business writing

Just like when we speak to someone, when we write, it is important to show interest in the person we are writing to. It makes a good impression.

Here are seven rules of polite writing and some language to accompany them.

1	Greet politely	Dear Abdul / Hi Abdul (*not just 'Abdul'*)
2	Thank for contact and/or open with a friendly statement	Thank you for your email / letter. (*when you reply to someone who has written to you*) / I hope you are well. / I hope things are going well.
3	Say you're happy to be in contact	Nice to hear from you. (*when you reply to someone who hasn't written for a long time*)
4	Congratulate on success	Congratulations on your promotion. Well done for getting the project completed on time.
5	Ask people, don't order them	Could I ask you a favour? Could you send me ...?
6	Say 'Thank you'	Thank you very much. / Thank you in advance. (*before you do what I ask*) / Thanks again for the (*information you sent me*). / Thanks and regards.
7	Sign off politely	Yours faithfully (*very formal*) Yours sincerely (*formal*) / Yours (*short form of Yours sincerely*) Best wishes (*friendly*) / Best (*short form of Best wishes*) Kind regards / Regards / Best regards (*friendly*)

Compare these two emails. Which one would you prefer to receive?

To: Bert
Subject: Updated figures
Bert, I need the updated figures for the first quarter ASAP. Thanks. Lucinda

To: Bert
Subject: Updated figures
Hi Bert, I hope you're well. Could you send me the updated figures for the first quarter as soon as possible, please? Thanks and regards, Lucinda

Writing task

Read the email on page 105 and then rewrite it.

Key take-aways

Write down the things you will take away from Unit 2 and how you will implement them.

Topic	Take-away	Implementation strategy – How?	Implementation time frame – When?
The four types of listener			
How to improve your listening skills with active listening			
How to build good relationships in conversation			
Using F.A.C.E. to show empathy			
How to build good relationships in business writing			

3 Small talk

Unimportant details can pave (open) the way to close relationships.

— Peter Menzies

Aims

- How to find things to talk about with different people
- Learn a 'small talk' format that works
- Learn how to avoid talking about things that can cause offence
- Learn about the cultural fault lines that divide people
- How to write a letter of apology after causing offence

A — How to start a conversation

Quiz

Small talk describes the conversations you have when you are not talking business.

It is the conversations before the meeting, in the staff restaurant or around the water cooler.

Do you agree or disagree with these statements? Tick Yes or No.

		Yes	No
1	I'm good at small talk in my own language.		
2	I'm good at small talk in English.		
3	I think the social aspect of doing business is very important.		
4	I think small talk wastes time before and in meetings. I prefer to get down to business straight away.		
5	I enjoy talking to people outside business meetings.		
6	I prefer listening and observing to talking.		
7	I find it difficult to choose things to talk about when socializing in English.		
8	I know what to talk about and what not to talk about when socializing in English.		

Briefing

It is important to get to know people personally. This is often the best way to build a good relationship and trust. The best time to do this is often outside the meeting, over coffee or at mealtimes.

WHAT you talk about is important. When you deal with other cultures there is a danger that you may cause offence. You may say the wrong thing, be too personal or ask something that is OK in your culture but not in theirs.

In addition, you may ask questions that fit cultural stereotypes. You may fix people wrongly in a traditional cultural image that your country has of them. It is important to see the people you deal with as PEOPLE, not as representatives of a cultural stereotype. How can you do this?

Recognize that everyone has different areas of experience. These influence the way they are. The five main areas of experience are:

- **National experience** – the country they come from
- **Regional experience** – the area in the country they come from
- **Professional experience** – the work or studies they have done and the organizations where they have worked
- **Social experience** – their experience of working in different organizations
- **Personal experience** – education and travel

You want to know more about the person you are dealing with but you don't want to cause offence. Are there neutral questions you can ask?

'Get to know Jo' is an exercise to help you find out more about the people you meet without causing offence. There are six questions. If you ask them and follow up their answers with other questions, it will help you understand more about the background of the person you are dealing with.

National experience	Where are you from?
Regional experience	What part of (*country*) are you from? What's it like there?
Professional experience	Where did you work before you worked here?
Social experience	How was your last job different?
Personal experience	Have you travelled or studied abroad?

What is important is not just the questions but the follow-up questions you can ask because of what you learn from the answers to the first questions. Notice that we have asked questions about country, region, work and travel. In many countries people prefer you not to talk about family and social background. That may be too personal.

Listening

14 | **1** | **Listen to five conversations and decide which type of experience they are about.**

- National experience
- Regional experience
- Professional experience
- Social experience
- Personal experience

Conversation	Experience
1	
2	
3	
4	
5	

14 | **2** | **Listen again to the five conversations and note down the follow-up questions.**

What other questions could you use as follow-up questions in these five conversations? Think about additional questions you might like to ask.

Business practice

15 | **1** | **Listen and repeat these questions.**

National experience	Where are you from?
	Where do you come from?
	Do you mind my / me asking where you are from?
Regional experience	What part are you from?
	What's special about your region?
Professional experience	What did you do before you came here?
	How long have you worked here?
	When did you start work here?
Social experience	How is this job different to / from your last one?
Personal experience	Do you have a holiday booked for this summer?
	Have you been to Morocco before?
	Where did you go to college?

2 **Test yourself. Cover the sentences opposite and then complete these sentences.**

1 Do you .... my asking where you are from?

2 What's .... about your region?

3 How .... have you worked here?

4 What did you do .... you came here?

5 .... you been there before?

6 How is this job different .... your last one?

3 **You are in a taxi with a new colleague. Ask questions to keep the conversation going. Then listen to the model conversation.**

You: *Ask about nationality.*

Colleague: I'm British. From Scotland, actually.

You: *Show interest. Ask what part.*

Colleague: I'm from Aberdeen. It's in the east of Scotland.

You: *Ask what is special about it.*

Colleague: Oh, it's the oil capital of Scotland. It's the centre of oil and gas drilling in the North Sea. I'm working there now.

You: *Show interest. Ask what your colleague did before this job.*

Colleague: Oh, before that I was at university in Edinburgh. I taught engineering.

You: *Ask how it was different.*

Colleague: Well, I was teaching students. Mainly Scottish. Now I'm working with oil and gas engineers from all over the world – especially from the US.

You: *Ask if your colleague has travelled a lot.*

Colleague: Yes, a lot. Too much really. I was in Mexico last week and Indonesia the week before. It's exhausting.

Business culture

Ice-breakers are topics that most people like to talk about. They may include sport, weather, families or general business. They are ways of 'breaking the ice' in a relationship.

However, it is also important to be sensitive to topics that different nationalities often prefer to avoid. We call these *ice-makers*. Discussing them makes the other person reluctant to talk to you.

Unfortunately, topics that are *ice-breakers* in your country may be *ice-makers* in somebody else's!

Look at the list of topics on page 105. Which ones are *ice-breakers* or *ice-makers* for you? Add notes to the table.

How to avoid causing offence

Briefing

In the *Business culture* section in 3A we looked at *ice-breakers* and *ice-makers*. Here we look at the cultural fault lines that can divide people from different societies.

In international business there are a number of sensitive areas that may be difficult to discuss. If you need or have to cross a cultural fault line, you must do so with great sensitivity. If you do not do so, you may offend your business partner and cause a breakdown in the working relationship.

In international business these are the main cultural fault lines to think about:

- Religious differences in a country
- Tensions between different language communities
- Regional differences
- Political differences
- Differences in economic status
- Differences in social status
- Historical rivalry with neighbouring countries
- Differences in the status of men and women

Glossary

A **fault line** in geology describes the plates of the surface of the earth. When they move, they can cause volcanoes, tsunamis and earthquakes. In a culture, fault lines can cause tension and conflict.

If you are visiting a country, it is important to find out about the cultural fault lines before you visit and to be sensitive when talking with people from that country.

Listening

17 **1** Sonia is at a conference party in a foreign country and is chatting to a local delegate. Listen and decide. Which fault lines does she cross?

1	Religious differences in a country	
2	Tensions between different language communities	
3	Regional differences	
4	Political differences	
5	Differences in economic status	
6	Differences in social status	
7	Historical rivalry with neighbouring countries	
8	Differences in the status of men and women	

2   **Listen again to Sonia's conversation with the delegate. Answer these questions.**

1   Does Sonia use any expressions to show she is sensitive to the cultural fault lines she crosses?

2   In your opinion was Sonia diplomatic enough in her questions?

3   In your opinion was the local delegate diplomatic in his answers?

4   At the end of the conversation do you think the delegate wanted to continue or finish the conversation?

Business practice

1   **Listen and repeat these sentences.**

How to ask about sensitive subjects	Do you mind if I ask you about the political situation? Would you mind if I asked you about the social problems here? Could I ask you a delicate question?
How to avoid difficult or sensitive subjects	I'd rather not discuss it if you don't mind. If you don't mind, I'd prefer not to talk about it. Can we change the subject?
How to agree to talk about a sensitive subject	Not at all. Go ahead. Feel free. No problem. What would you like to know?
How to apologize if you raise a sensitive area in conversation	I'm sorry if I said the wrong thing. I'm sorry. I didn't mean to cause offence. I'm afraid I may have caused offence. If so, I'm sorry.

2   **Test yourself. Cover the sentences above and then complete these sentences.**

1   .... you mind if I asked about the position of women in your company?

2   .... you mind if I ask about the fighting in the north?

3   If you don't ...., I'd rather not talk about the political situation.

4   I'm .... if I said the wrong thing.

5   No ....

6   Can we change the ....?

🎧 **3**

19

You are having a drink with John, a business partner, after work and need to find out the answers to some questions that you know may cross a cultural fault line. Ask the questions to find out what you need to know sensitively. Then listen to the model conversation.

You: *Ask John if you can ask about a sensitive subject, the political situation.*

John: Feel free. What would you like to know?

You: *Ask John your follow-up question. You have heard that the President's brother is a paid consultant of John's company.*

John: Ah, I'd rather not discuss that if you don't mind.

You: *Apologize for asking the question.*

John: Don't worry about it.

You: *Say you'd like to ask another question.*

John: Go on.

You: *Ask where you and John are having dinner tonight.*

John: That's much easier to answer!

Business writing

Sometimes you need to write an email or letter to apologize for a mistake you have made if you have caused offence. How do you do it? Remember these four steps of apology.

Paragraph 1	**Pleasure**	Say it was a pleasure to see the person.
Paragraph 2	**Problem**	Describe the problem.
Paragraph 3	**Explanation and apology**	Explain and apologize for any rudeness.
Paragraph 4	**Intention**	Say what will happen in the future.

Writing task

1   Read the letter opposite and answer these questions.

1 What was the invitation?

2 What does the visitor think he may have done wrong?

3 What is normal in his country?

4 What does he think may not be normal in his host's country?

5 How does he apologize?

6 What does he want to do in the future?

Dear _____ ,

It was a great pleasure to see you again and thank you so much for the invitation to your lovely home and the delicious meal.

I am concerned that during the meal I may have caused offence in asking questions about your wife and family. Please excuse me if I did.

It is normal, as you know, to ask about partners and families in my country and I just did the same thing in your house. I'm sorry if I said the wrong thing. I didn't mean to cause offence and I hope you will understand.

Thank you again for the wonderful evening and I look forward to returning your hospitality and seeing you soon.

Regards,

Simon

2 **Now write a similar letter based on a situation where you think you may have caused offence.**

Key take-aways

Write down the things you will take away from Unit 3 and how you will implement them.

Topic	Take-away	Implementation strategy – How?	Implementation time frame – When?
Understand the five key areas of cultural experience			
Learn how to avoid stereotypes			
Learn a 'small talk' format that works			
Understand ice-breakers and ice-makers			
Learn about cultural fault lines			
How to write a letter of apology after causing offence			

4 Presentation organization

Tell them what you are going to say, tell them you are saying it. Then tell them you have said it. — Winston Churchill

Aims
- How to signpost, signal and summarize during a presentation
- How to use the **Three Ss** technique
- How to respond to and answer questions
- How to deal with interruptions
- How to structure a short written report

A | How to structure your presentation

Quiz

What kind of presenter are you? Tick Yes, No or Sometimes.

		Yes	No	Sometimes
1	I work best with a prepared speech, which I read out.			
2	I present best by speaking from notes.			
3	I present best when I have a slide presentation.			
4	I present best when I speak naturally, without using slides.			
5	I prefer to speak from a lectern so I can see my speech.			
6	I prefer to have no barrier between me and the audience.			
7	I prefer talking to the audience without interaction.			
8	I prefer interacting with the audience.			
9	I always ask the audience to leave their questions till the end of my presentation.			
10	I encourage my audience to interrupt and ask questions at any time.			

Briefing

Everybody in business has to make presentations at some point. A business presentation may be an informal three-minute report to colleagues in a meeting or a formal 45-minute speech to a large group of people you have never met before. But every presentation can have the same structure.

Learn this structure and it will be much easier to make your presentations:

- Tell them what you are going to say.
- Tell them you are saying it.
- Tell them you have said it.

Think of your presentation as a story. It has a beginning, a middle and an end. At the beginning tell your audience what you are going to say. In the middle tell your audience you are saying it. At the end tell your audience you have said it. To do this, use the Three Ss technique: SIGNPOST, SIGNAL and SUMMARIZE.

Signpost

- Tell the audience your topic.
- Tell them how long the presentation will last.
- Tell them the main points you will make.
- Tell them if and when they can ask questions.

Signal

- Tell the audience when you are beginning each point.
- Tell the audience when you have finished each point.
- Your audience will know where you are in your presentation and this avoids confusion.

Summarize

- Summarize your main points.
- Make a conclusion. For example, what should we learn from the presentation?
- Invite questions.

Listening

1 Listen to a presentation about migration in the European Union and identify where each of the Three Ss starts and finishes. Listen again and check your answers in the Audio script.

2 Listen again to the presentation and complete these sentences.

1 I'm .... to talk about the international migration of labour.

2 If you have any questions, please feel free to ....

3 My first .... is why migration is a problem.

4 I have .... three points.

5 Thank you for ....

6 If there are any questions, I'll be .... to answer them.

Business practice

 1   **Listen and repeat these phrases.**

Signposting phrases

Title
> My presentation is entitled …
>
> I'd like to talk about the current project.
>
> I'd like to give you an update on my current project.

Duration
> My presentation will last about three minutes.
>
> I'll talk for about three minutes.

Main points
> I'll make three main points: first …, second … and finally …

Questions
> If you have any questions, please feel free to interrupt.
>
> If you have any questions, I'll be happy to answer them at the end.

Signalling phrases
> My first point is …
>
> That was my first point.
>
> My second point is …
>
> That was my second point.
>
> My final point is …
>
> That was my final point.

Summarizing phrases

Summary
> In this presentation I have made three main points. First …, second … and finally …

Conclusion
> In conclusion, I think …
>
> That is the end of my presentation.
>
> Thank you for listening.

Questions
> If you have any questions, I'll be happy to answer them now.
>
> If there are any questions, I'll be pleased to answer them.
>
> Any questions? (*informal*)

Thanking
> Thank you.
>
> Thanks for your attention.

2 **Test yourself. Cover the sentences opposite and then complete the sentences with words from the box.**

If	conclusion	last	entitled	answer	would

1 If you have any questions, I will be pleased to .... them.

2 In ...., I think we have to choose the Belmont site for the office.

3 My presentation will .... about 15 minutes.

4 My presentation is .... *How we go and stay green*.

5 I .... like to give you an update on the project.

6 .... you have any questions, please feel free to interrupt.

3 **Prepare your own presentation.**

Think of a work topic. Make notes. Write down:

- The topic
- The three main points you want to make

Then practise introducing your topic. Remember the four things you have to do.

- Title
- Duration
- Main points
- Questions

Take your first point. Write three things about it. Then practise.

- Introduce it with a signalling phrase.
- Finish it with a signalling phrase.

Now write a summary. Remember these four points:

- Summary (*your key points*)
- Conclusion (*why it's important*)
- Questions (*invite questions*)
- Thanks (*thank the audience for listening*)

4 **Deliver your presentation. Make it about one to two minutes long. Record it and then play it back. If possible, ask a friend or colleague to review and comment on it.**

Focus on these points:

- Did you include all the **signposts** (title, duration, main points, questions)?
- Did you include the **signalling** points (introducing and closing each point)?
- Did you include the **summarizing** points (summary, conclusion, questions, thanks)?

Business culture

See the questionnaire on page 106 and answer the questions about what *you* expect from a presentation and what other people expect.

How to deal with questions and interruptions

Briefing

Here we look at how to answer questions *during* and *at the end of* a presentation, and how to deal with interruptions.

To answer questions, use the Four Answers technique:

1	Thank
2	Repeat
3	Answer
4	Check

Why use the Four Answers?

Thanking the questioner is polite and makes them feel good. Repeating the question gives you time to think. It also allows you to rephrase the question to make sure you have understood it correctly. It also gives you the opportunity to make sure everyone in the audience has heard the question. When you have answered the question, ask if the question has been answered sufficiently.

How to stop interruptions

If someone interrupts you and you want to finish your sentence, politely ask them to let you finish what you want to say first. Keep control of your presentation. Don't let members of the audience take control.

What to say when you don't know the answer

If you are part of a team, refer the question to a member of the team who does know the answer. If more information is available on your website, refer the questioner to the website. Offer to get back to the questioner later with an answer.

Listening

🎧 **22** **1** Listen to the question and answer session at the end of the presentation you heard in 4A. Which of these things does the presenter do?

Question 1		Question 2	
• Thank	☐	• Thank	☐
• Repeat	☐	• Repeat	☐
• Answer	☐	• Answer	☐
• Check	☐	• Check	☐
• Refer to team or website	☐	• Refer to team or website	☐
• Offer to contact questioner	☐	• Offer to contact questioner	☐

2 **Listen to the question and answer session again, and answer these questions.**

1 The questioner interrupts. How does the speaker stop him interrupting?

2 How does the questioner indicate he wants to ask a supplementary question?

3 The speaker isn't sure she has completely understood the second question. What phrase does she use to indicate this?

4 How does she express regret that she doesn't know the answer?

Business practice

1 **Listen and repeat the sentences.**

Thanking and repeating	Thank you for the question.
	The question was ...
	If I understand, you want to know ...
	If I understood correctly, the question was ...
Answering and checking	The answer is ...
	Does that answer your question?
Dealing with interruptions	Please, just let me finish.
	If I could just finish what I was going to say.
	Can I answer that question at the end of the presentation?
	Could we deal with that at the end of the presentation?
Saying you don't know the answer	I'm afraid I don't have the answer to hand.
	Can anybody in my team answer that question?
	Can I refer you to our website?
	If you give me your details after the presentation, I'll get back to you.

2 **Test yourself. Cover the sentences above and then complete these sentences.**

1 If I have .... correctly, the question was this.

2 I'm .... I don't have the answer.

3 If you give me your email address, I'll get .... to you.

4 Could I .... you to our website?

5 Can anyone in my .... help me here?

6 Could we .... with that at the end?

3 **You are at the end of your presentation and ready to take questions. Listen and respond. Then listen to the model conversation.**

You: *Say you have finished. Ask if there are questions.*

Questioner: Yes, I have a question about costs. How can you be sure you can keep to budget?

You: *Thank, repeat question, answer it and check.*

Questioner: Well, I'm not convinced. I think you'll go over over budget.

You: *Offer to make information available to audience member after the presentation is over.*

Questioner: Thanks. That would be very useful. I have another question.

You: *Acknowledge the question.*

Questioner: What happens if you do go over budget?

You: *Say you are confident that will not happen. Check you have answered the question.*

Questioner: Yes, thanks.

Business writing

The Three Ss technique you saw in 4A can also be applied to short reports. However, we use different titles.

Introduction	Title, what the topic is about, summary of main points and / or recommendations.
Main points	Three main points; introduce sub-points if you wish. Allow a new paragraph for each new point. If there are a lot of sub-points, start each new point with a heading.
Conclusion and recommendations	Summarize the points you have made, say why they are important, include recommendations.

Writing task

1 **Read the report opposite.**

1 What are the main points

2 Which paragraphs explain the main points?

3 What is the conclusion?

4 Is the report clear?

Helping migrant workers harmonize relations in the workplace

Summary of project update

Summary

The project committee wishes to source funding to provide support for management and human resources to help new workers from other countries work successfully with local staff. Three things will help us do this: research, training and training materials.

Research

We propose to research the problems of migrant workers in six key industries and sectors: transport, health, food and drink, education, construction and manufacturing. From this we will be able to identify key issues we need to address in training and training materials.

Training

We propose two types of courses. The first is a workshop for staff to meet each other in order to discuss and harmonize differences. The second is a train-the-trainer certificate that trains teachers and human resources managers to use the training materials and deliver the training.

Training materials

We propose to produce a self-study set of training materials to help both local and new migrant staff understand and harmonize the differences between them. We suggest the best way to do this is to produce a video of typical situations, a training manual and a trainer's manual to help colleagues understand typical problems and resolve them. We also plan to have an online programme for staff who cannot attend face-to-face training sessions.

Conclusion and recommendations

Research shows that the number of migrant workers will increase significantly in the next few years. It is important for companies to train their staff in how to work best with new workers from other countries. To do this we propose the following training programme and training materials:

1 Research into six key industries / sectors
2 Development of a training programme and certificate for trainers
3 Development of video and print training materials for face-to-face and online training

2 Use this model to write a short report on a business activity you have been involved with in the last six months.

Key take-aways

Write down the things you will take away from Unit 4 and how you will implement them.

Topic	Take-away	Implementation strategy – How?	Implementation time frame – When?
The **Three Ss** technique			
Common phrases for presentations and questions			
How to deal with questions			
How to deal with interruptions			
How to adapt the **Three Ss** technique to a written report			

5 Preparation and delivery

Poor preparation means poor performance.

Aims

- How to prepare for an international presentation
- How to manage international expectations of presentations
- How to deal with nerves before and during a presentation
- How to do a team presentation
- How to prepare visuals for an international audience

A How to prepare

Quiz

How effective a presenter are you?
Tick Yes, No or Sometimes.

		Yes	No	Sometimes
1	Do you spend enough time on preparing your presentation?			
2	Do you rehearse your presentation, either alone or in front of a colleague or colleagues?			
3	Do you prepare your own visuals or do you get someone to help you do this?			
4	Do you get nervous before presentations?			
5	If you get nervous, do you use any techniques for reducing those nerves?			
6	Do you research the needs, desires and make-up of your audience before you present to them?			
7	Do you always present on your own, or do you present as part of a team?			
8	If you present in teams, do you enjoy that? Or do you prefer to present on your own?			
9	Do you say hello to members of your audience if they arrive early? Do you try to find out something about them?			
10	Do you prefer to say nothing until you start your presentation?			

Glossary

The **make-up** of something consists of its different parts and the way these parts are arranged.

Briefing

All good presenters do two things before any presentation. They prepare and they practise.

Here are some tips to help you prepare and practise your presentation. First, we'll go through three key principles in turn:

- Know what you want to achieve
- Know how to organize
- Know your audience

Know what you want to achieve

Most presenters want to do at least one of these things in a presentation:

- Exchange information (you might do this when updating colleagues on progress)
- Change behaviour (you might do this in a motivational presentation)
- Sell a product or service

Know how to organize

We have already focused on the Three Ss technique for presentations in 4A. Here are five other things to think about:

1 **Message** Summarize the key message of the presentation in one sentence. This is what you want your audience to remember as a result of your presentation. Use it at the beginning and end of your presentation.

2 **Main point(s)** Decide on three main points that will develop your key message. These will be the main points in your Three Ss structure.

3 **Motivation** Ask yourself: *Why will my audience be interested in this?*

4 **Take-aways** What will your audience take away from your presentation? Emphasize the take-away value in your summary.

5 **Examples** Can you think of any memorable short stories or anecdotes to tell to illustrate your points?

Know your audience

Try to find out something about your audience before you meet them online or face-to-face. Use the acronym AUDIENCE to help you find what to research.

A	Audience	How many? From where?
U	Understand	What do they know already?
D	Demographic	Age, gender, social background, professions
I	Interests	What do they want to know?
E	Environment	Will they all be able to hear and see me easily?
N	Needs	What are their needs?
C	Customize	How do I need to adapt my presentation to their needs?
E	Expectations	What do my audience expect to learn or hear?

Remember these principles and use them with the Three Ss structure when you plan your presentations.

Together with these principles, good presenters use four techniques to keep their audience listening:

1 **Hooking** A hook catches a fish. It also catches the attention of the audience. What is your hook?

2 **Flagging** Tell your audience what is important.

3 **Bridging** Make a clear bridge between your points.

4 **Looping** Refer back to a point you made earlier in the presentation in order to reinforce it.

Listening

 1 **Listen to the start of a presentation about the future of energy resources and answer the questions.**

1 What is the presenter's key message?
2 What are the presenter's main points?
3 What is the audience's motivation for listening to the presentation?
4 How does the presenter illustrate his message?
5 How does he loop?

2 **Listen again and complete these sentences.**

1 Can you .... a world without energy?
2 So .... do we manage and develop our energy resources better?
3 Well, the first .... we have to do is to conserve our energy resources better.
4 The second thing I want to .... is we have to develop new forms of energy.
5 The third point I want to make is that managing and developing energy resources is .... at three levels: economically, socially and personally.
6 So, ... back to where our company comes in ...

Business practice

1 **Listen and repeat these sentences.**

Hooking – getting the audience's attention	Let me tell you how to increase your profits.
	I'd like to offer some ideas on how to increase productivity.
	I want to share with you my experience in the financial markets.
	Imagine a world where you couldn't use your mobile phone. What would you do?
	Can you imagine a world where you couldn't use your mobile phone?

Flagging – emphasizing what's important	This is a really crucial point. This is the most important point I want to make. This is vitally important. Make no mistake. This really matters.
Bridging – linking one point to another	Another important point is motivation. Following that, we need to discuss how to engage our staff. Let me turn now to my next point. This brings me to my final point, what needs to change and how.
Looping – reinforcing what you have said before	As I said earlier, motivation is very important. You may remember I mentioned motivation. I said I would discuss efficiency savings. This is the right moment to do so. Coming back to what I said before …

2 **Prepare your own presentation.**

Think of a work topic. Make notes. Write down:

- your main message
- the points that will develop the message
- your audience's motivation for listening to you
- a hook for your audience
- the take-away value for your audience

Now think how you will:

- flag what is important
- bridge points
- loop back to points

3 **Deliver your presentation. Make it one to two minutes long.**

Record it and then play it back. If possible, ask a friend or colleague to review and comment on it.

Focus on these points:

- Did you get your main points across clearly?
- Did you find a good hook to get the audience's attention?
- Did you link the parts of your presentation carefully?

Business culture

People in different parts of the world have different expectations of a presentation. As we have said, the important thing is to know and / or research what your audience is expecting. See pages 106 and 107 and read about six common challenges you might face.

Briefing

Many presenters are nervous when they present. And when English is not your first language, it can make you very nervous, especially if you worry about making mistakes. But remember: *your audience wants you to do well!*

How to overcome nerves before you present

- Try out the room. Many presenters get to the presentation place early to try out the room. They stand or sit where they will present. They also stand or sit where the audience will be.
- Check sound, check vision. Can the audience hear you? Can they see you? If another person (e.g. a technician) is in the presentation room, check they can hear you and see you from different positions.
- Check the equipment. Make sure any equipment you are using is working OK and make sure you know how to use it. If you are not sure, ask the technician (if one is available) to be on standby during your presentation.
- Say hello to 'early birds'. Some people always arrive early. Welcome them. Introduce yourself. Ask them about themselves. Ask them why they have come and what they want to get from the session.
- Breathe. When we are nervous, we forget to breathe. Take a minute before you start and breathe in (four seconds), hold your breath (four seconds), breathe out (four seconds). Do this three times. It will help you relax.
- Visualize. Shut your eyes. Make a mental image of yourself. You are confident. You know what you are talking about. Your audience is interested. Visualize yourself doing well.

And when you present to the audience

- Take charge of the space. Don't just stay in one space. Move around a bit but not so much that it becomes distracting.
- Don't just read your notes or the presentation slide content aloud. Read, look up, speak.
- Make eye contact. Don't just stare at the back of the room. Make eye contact with every part of the audience briefly as you present.
- Gesture. Show you are alive. Use your arms and hands to emphasize key points.

And, if you can, present with colleagues to take away some of the stress of presenting. Presenting in teams requires extra preparation and good organization but it can make your presentations more dynamic and convincing. And fun.

Listening

1 **Listen to Kirsten and Sue presenting the new company intranet to colleagues in their company. Answer the questions.**

1 Describe Kirsten and Sue's presentation style. Is it lively or dull?

2 Do the two presenters sound as if they work together or separately? What makes you think this?

3 Who does each part of the presentation? Put a tick in the box under the name.

Part	Kirsten	Sue
Introduction to the site		
Details of what you can do on the new site		
How you can put content on the new site		

4 How does Kirsten hook the audience?

2 **Listen again and complete these sentences.**

1 There's a special new feature on it which I know you're going to ....

2 .... to you, Sue.

3 To find out how to visit the new site, let me .... you back to Kirsten.

4 Kirsten, ... to you again.

5 Thanks a lot and we'll look .... to hearing from you.

Business practice

1 **Listen and repeat these sentences.**

Saying who will do what	This will be a joint presentation. This is Sue Brown, who will be presenting with me. I will introduce the topic. Sue and I will present the main points. Finally. I will sum up.
Handing over	Let me hand over to Sue for the first main point. Kirsten, back to you again. Over to you, Sue.
Handing back	Let me hand you back to Kirsten. Sue, the floor is yours. It's all yours, Kirsten.

2 Test yourself. Complete these sentences.

1   Let me hand .... to Sue for the first point.

2   The floor is ....

3   This will be a .... presentation.

4   .... me hand you back to Sue.

3 You're doing a joint presentation with Tomas Schmidt about your company's new training programme. Start the presentation. Then listen to the model presentation.

You: *Welcome the audience, state the purpose of the presentation and introduce Tomas Schmidt.*

Tomas: Good morning, everyone.

You: *Say you will introduce the programme and that Tomas will give the details.*

Tomas: Yes, I'll give the details afterwards.

You: *Introduce the programme. State its purpose is to increase productivity at the same time as job satisfaction* (this is the hook). *Hand over to Tomas.*

Tomas: Thank you. Here are the details. The programme will be modular and will run over a period of 12 months. In liaison with your line manager, you choose the parts of the course that are best for you. There are ten and you must do at least five. The parts cover things like Working in teams and Time management. OK, so back to you.

You: *Thank Tomas. Say you want to look in more detail at the reasons for the programme. Direct the audience to your slide.*

Business writing

What do your slides look like? Most presenters use slides (PowerPoint or a similar software application) in their presentations. Read the nine guidelines opposite for making a slide.

Remember: if the audience can't read it, don't show it!

A lot of print that they can't read is useless to your audience and is frustrating for them. If you have to say *You probably can't see this very well ...*, then you shouldn't show it.

Writing task

Use your computer and prepare your own slide. Practise using the nine rules.

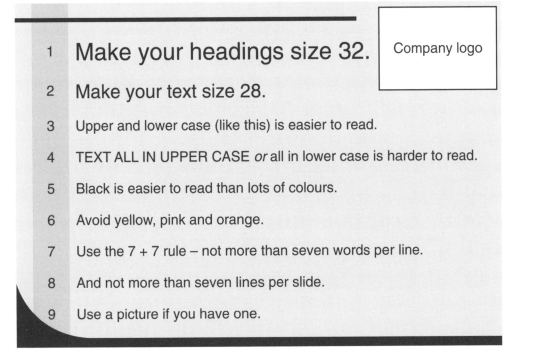

1. Make your headings size 32.

   Company logo

2. Make your text size 28.

3. Upper and lower case (like this) is easier to read.

4. TEXT ALL IN UPPER CASE *or* all in lower case is harder to read.

5. Black is easier to read than lots of colours.

6. Avoid yellow, pink and orange.

7. Use the 7 + 7 rule – not more than seven words per line.

8. And not more than seven lines per slide.

9. Use a picture if you have one.

Key take-aways

Write down the things you will take away from Unit 5 and how you will implement them.

Topic	Take-away	Implementation strategy – How?	Implementation time frame – When?
The three principles of a presentation			
How to analyse your audience			
How to use hooking, flagging, bridging and looping			
How to find out an international audience's expectations			
How to deal with nerves			
The language of a joint presentation			
How to prepare a slide presentation			

6 Presentation style

There are always three speeches for every one you actually gave. The one you practised, the one you gave, and the one you wish you gave.

— Dale Carnegie

Aims

- How to use effective presentation delivery techniques
- How to adapt your style for maximum clarity
- How to use your voice and visuals
- How to make sure your delivery is clear
- How to write thank you letters to presenters and organizers

A Presentation delivery techniques

Quiz

What is your presentation style? Tick the boxes which are closest to your natural style of presentation.

1	**Direct** I am direct. I say what I think.	
2	**Indirect** I am indirect. I prefer to avoid conflict.	
3	**Details** I need facts and details.	
4	**Suggestions** I prefer to offer a general outline.	
5	**What / Why** I make my point first and then I explain it in more detail and give examples.	
6	**Why / What** I like to explain the background context and then summarize the point I want to make.	
7	**Formal** I believe a formal style is appropriate in a presentation.	
8	**Informal** I prefer a relaxed friendly style.	
9	**Emotional** I think it is important to show my emotions.	
10	**Neutral** I think it is important to keep my emotions to myself.	
11	**Fast** I usually speak quite fast when I present.	
12	**Slow** My natural presentation style is slow and measured.	

Briefing

There are six presentation delivery techniques you can use to get your audience's attention. These are especially effective at the beginning and end of your presentation.

1	Ask a rhetorical question	Begin your presentation with a question which introduces and illustrates your key message. You answer it yourself and at the end you repeat the question (we saw this in action in 5A).
2	Make a contrast	Contrast two things. Always start with the negative, for example *It's not this, it's THIS!*
3	Repeat for emphasis	Repeat key words and phrases to emphasize key points. Remember US President Obama's *Yes, we can.*
4	Sell an experience	Put the audience in a situation which brings alive the point you want to make, for example by talking about a relevant personal experience.
5	Make important points in groups of three	This technique helps the audience memorize what you want them to remember and take away from the presentation.
6	Surprise addition	Give your audience a bonus. Offer one more idea or suggestion at the end of your presentation.

Listening

1 A tour operator is giving a presentation to a group of travel agents about holidays in Croatia. Listen to her presentation. Which of the six techniques does she use?

Tick the techniques you hear.

Ask a question	Make a contrast	Repeat for emphasis	Sell an experience	Group points in threes	Just one more thing

2 Listen to the talk again. This time put the techniques in the order the presenter uses them.

Ask a question	Make a contrast	Repeat for emphasis	Sell an experience	Group points in threes	Just one more thing

Business practice

🎧 31

1 Listen and repeat these sentences.

Ask a rhetorical question	Let me start with a question. How do you engage your staff?
	Let me ask a question at this point. How many of us do overtime on a regular basis?
Make a contrast	It's not what you do. It's the way that you do it that counts in this business.
	You don't just come for sun. You come for culture and history and fun!
Repeat key messages	So let me repeat one more time, turnover is vanity, profit is sanity.
	Remember, timing is everything.
	One thing is important in presentations – practise, practise and practise again.
Sell an experience	Let me show you how this works.
	I'm going to show you how good this idea is.
	Let me tell you about a real-life experience.
	Let me take you on a journey.
Say things in threes	So let me summarize. Revenue up, costs down, gross margin up.
	Remember the Three Ss: signpost, signal, summarize.
	Here are three things you can be sure of.
Surprise additions	And one more thing …
	Before I finish, let me offer you one more idea …
	I'd like to offer you one final thought …
	One final thought before we finish …

2 Here are some famous quotations. What technique does each one demonstrate?

1 *Ask not what your country can do for you. Ask what you can do for your country.*   John F. Kennedy

2 *Veni, vidi, vici. I came, I saw, I conquered.*   Julius Caesar

3 *Oh, and just one more thing …*   Steve Jobs

4 *Famous entrepreneur Richard Branson was once asked: 'What does Virgin stand for?' He could have answered 'a great music store' or 'a great airline', but instead he answered with one word – 'fun'.*   Carmine Gallo

5 *Watch your thoughts; they become words.*

Watch your words; they become actions.

Watch your actions; they become habits.

Watch your habits; they become character.

Watch your character; it becomes your destiny.   Lao Tsu

6 *To be or not to be? That is the question.*   William Shakespeare

3 **Prepare your own presentation.**

- Choose two or three of the presentation delivery techniques that you feel comfortable with.

- Choose a topic you are interested in.

- Prepare a one- to two-minute presentation using the presentation techniques.

4 **Deliver your presentation. Record it and then play it back. If possible, ask a friend or colleague to review and comment on it.**

Focus on your use of the presentation delivery techniques. Did you use them successfully?

Business culture

When you are giving a presentation in a foreign language, you can sometimes be difficult to understand. Use these five techniques to make it easier for your audience to understand you.

1 **A-r-t-i-c-u-l-a-t-e.** Speak a little slower than you usually would.

2 **Pause** before names, dates, figures, places and events – it makes them easier to understand. Try saying your name, for example *My name is (pause) Jaime (pause) Guerrero.*

3 **Avoid idiomatic or colloquial expressions.** If you have to use them, explain them, for example *As the chairman said, we have to start again from scratch, so we'll start again from the beginning.*

4 **Spell out acronyms and initials.** For example, say *I work in Customer Relations Management* not *I work in CRM.* Don't assume your audience knows the acronyms and initials.

5 **KISS – Keep It Short and Simple.** Short sentences with one thought per sentence are easier to understand than longer ones with lots of different ideas in them. If you can, keep your sentences to about 12 words.

If you use these five techniques, your presentations will be clearer and easier to follow.

Voice and visuals

Briefing

You have prepared your presentation. You have introduced some interesting delivery techniques. Now you need to focus on two things. How do you use your voice? How do you use visuals in your presentation?

Here are nine things that good presenters do.

Voice

1	Breathe before speaking	Your pitch is the tone of your voice. A very high voice can be hard to listen to. A very deep voice can be difficult to understand. If you breathe before you speak, your voice usually has a more level pitch. It also helps to breathe before you speak if you are nervous. If you are tense, your voice is usually higher than normal.
2	Stress important words	Remember that in English we stress the most important word in the sentence. Listen to the recordings which accompany this book and note how the speakers stress important words.
3	Vary your speed	Don't speak at exactly the same speed all the time. Slow down for really important points.
4	Vary the volume	Speak more softly when you want to share something personal. Speak louder to emphasize your key points.
5	Pause for effect	Use silence for dramatic effect. Don't be afraid to pause before you emphasize an important point or after you have made one. It gives the audience time to prepare for or to absorb the information.

Visuals

6	Face the audience	Talk to the audience not to the visuals or your notes.
7	Don't hide the visuals	Don't stand in front of the projector, screen or flipchart. If you write on a flipchart or whiteboard, let the audience see what you are writing.
8	Point	Use a pointer or your finger to highlight what you are referring to in your visuals. The audience needs to know where to look.
9	Talk about the visuals	Your audience can read. Don't just repeat what is on the screen or the flipchart. Refer to it, say what it shows and discuss the implications and not the text itself.

And remember: if your audience can't see what you are showing them because the image or print size is too small, DON'T SHOW IT.

Listening

1 Listen to an internal company presentation about video-conferencing. Tick the things the presenter does.

Stresses important information	
Uses silence	
Varies speed	
Varies volume	
Pauses for effect	
Refers to the slide	
Repeats what is on the slide	

2 Listen to the presentation again and complete these sentences.

1 I want to talk today about the company's plans to make video-conferencing the .... way we have international meetings.

2 Have a .... at this slide on costs.

3 This .... total employee hours in the air.

4 So my main .... is this.

5 What we .... to do is two things.

Business practice

1 Listen and repeat these sentences.

Introduce a visual	Have a look at this slide.
	Let me show you this slide.
	Look at the flipchart.
Describe what is on the slide	This slide shows ...
	If you look at this slide, you can see ...
	As you can see from the slide, ...
Stress important points	So my main point is ...
	The reason why this is important is ...
	The important thing to remember is that ...

Pause for effect	So my main point is this. [*pause*] The amount of air travel is not an efficient use of our resources or our time.
	What's the conclusion? [*pause*] It's obvious.
	The first point is [*pause*] the benefit to our customers.

2 **Prepare your own presentation.**

- Go back to the presentation you did in 6A. If you recorded it, listen to it again. Did you use your voice effectively?

- Plan to do your presentation again, this time referring to a visual: a slide or flipchart sheet.

- Prepare to give your presentation again and think about where you will pause, speak louder or slower, and use silence for effect. Think also how you will comment on the visual.

3 **Deliver your presentation. Record it and then play it back. If possible, ask a friend or colleague to review and comment on it.**

1 Focus on how you use your voice. Did you use it better than in 6A?

2 Focus on how you use your visual. Did you comment on it clearly?

Business writing

How do you thank a presenter after the presentation? Here is an example.

To:	Tony
From:	Jackie
Subject:	Presenting to Board

Dear Tony,

Thank you for agreeing to come and present to the Board of directors. The session went very well and the feedback was very positive.

Thank you again for taking the time.

Kind regards,

Jackie

And how do you respond? Read this example.

To:	Jackie
From:	Tony
Subject:	Presenting to Board

Dear Jackie,

Thank you for your email and for inviting me to give the presentation to the Board.

I'm glad it went well and I was very pleased to have the opportunity.

It was also a great pleasure to see you and to work with you.

Thank you again for thinking of me and I hope to have the pleasure of working with you again soon.

Regards,

Tony

Writing task

Think of a presentation someone has asked you to make. Or imagine someone has invited you to make a presentation to a large professional conference. Write a letter of thanks to the organizer.

Key take-aways

Write down the things you will take away from Unit 6 and how you will implement them.

Topic	Take-away	Implementation strategy – How?	Implementation time frame – When?
Presentation delivery techniques			
How to adapt your communication style			
How to use your voice and visuals			
How to make sure your delivery is clear			
How to write thank-you letters to presenters and organizers			

7 Running a successful meeting

Did we make a decision in there?

— US executive after a meeting in Britain

Aims

- How to prepare an agenda
- How to run a meeting
- How to understand what people expect from a meeting
- Tips for chairing meetings
- How to write the minutes of a meeting

A Setting the agenda

Quiz

How do you feel about the meetings you attend?

How are the meetings run?

Read the statements and choose Yes or No.

		Yes	No
1	I have too many meetings.		
2	The meetings are too long.		
3	We always have an agenda for the meeting.		
4	We usually have just one point for discussion.		
5	We always have a chair to control the meeting.		
6	The chair is always the most senior person present.		
7	We always have clear outcomes from our meetings.		
8	I often don't know what we have agreed at the end of a meeting.		
9	We keep full records of what people said in our meetings.		
10	We only record things we have agreed to do.		

Briefing

Many business people would say that they have to attend too many meetings and that meetings often last too long. How can we:

- make them shorter?
- get clear results and outcomes?
- ensure participation by everyone who attends?

There are three key factors for a successful meeting:

- Agenda
- Minutes
- Control

Here we'll look at the agenda. We'll deal with minutes and control in 7B.

Agenda

An agenda is a written order of the things you want to discuss, including the details shown here. A clear agenda that you don't change is the simplest way to make a meeting effective.

When the meeting is, how long the meeting is, who is invited. ·········· **Staff meeting**

Staff meeting
Date
Time and duration
Participants
AGENDA
Apologies for absence
Minutes of the last meeting
Matters arising
Agenda items
1
2
3
AOB (any other business)
Date of next meeting

When the meeting is, how long the meeting is, who is invited.

It is important to tell people in advance if you can't attend a meeting.

Participants should receive these before the meeting.

This is an opportunity to check that action points in the minutes have been carried out, and, if not, why not.

These are listed and discussed in order.

Anything else that needs to be discussed.

Agree when the next meeting will take place.

You can also use this format for a conference call. This agenda is quite formal, but even in informal meetings there will usually be a list of agenda items to discuss.

Think of your last meeting. Did it include all these points? If not, was there a good reason to exclude them?

Would meetings be better if you included them all?

Listening

34 **1** Listen to a company meeting about organizing a staff party. The Chair, Amy, Frances and Tony are present. Look at the agenda. What decisions were made as a result of the discussion about the agenda items? Make notes on the agenda. At the end of the meeting there are two items of AOB. What are they? When is the date of the next meeting?

AGENDA
Agenda items – Staff party
1 Where to hold event ....
2 Who to invite ....
3 Budget for event ....
4 Inviting a special guest ....
AOB (any other business)
AOB 1 ....
AOB 2 ....
Date of next meeting ....

34 **2** Listen again and complete these sentences.

1 Thank you for ....

2 George sends his ....

3 Let's take the .... as read.

4 Any .... thoughts on that?

5 Everyone .... then?

Business practice

35 **1** Listen and repeat these sentences.

Start the meeting	Thank you for joining the meeting.
	Shall we start the meeting now?
	Let's kick off, shall we? (*informal*)
Introduce participants	Let's go round the table and introduce ourselves. (*if people don't know each other*)
Apologies	Sue sends her apologies.
Minutes	Jan, could you take the minutes?
	Has everyone read the minutes of the last meeting?
Matters arising from the minutes	Are there any matters arising?
	Can we take the minutes as read?

Agenda items	Let's move on to the agenda.
	Item 1.
	Could you speak about that, Tom?
Noting results	Could you minute that?
	Let's minute that.
AOB	Any other business? Let's go round the table.
Date of next meeting	Let's agree the date of the next meeting. Same time, same place next month?
Close	Thank you very much everybody.
	Can you send me the minutes and I'll circulate them?

2 Test yourself. Cover the sentences opposite and then complete these sentences.

1 Can someone .... the minutes?

2 Let's go .... the table and introduce ourselves.

3 Let's .... off the meeting, shall we?

4 Can you .... me the minutes and I'll circulate them?

5 Are there any matters ....?

3 You are chairing a short meeting with your colleagues Elena, Tom and John. Follow the instructions. Then listen to the model conversation.

You: *Thank everyone for coming. Ask someone to take the minutes.*

Elena: I'll do it.

You: *Thank Elena. Ask John to speak about item 1 on the agenda, last month's sales figures.*

John: Well, we were slightly ahead of budget and took a good order from a big supermarket chain. Nothing else to report really.

You: *Thank John. Ask for what John said to be minuted. Then ask Elena to speak about item 2, the recruitment of the new IT director.*

Elena: Well, it's proving very difficult. We've decided to use a specialist recruitment company to find someone.

You: *Acknowledge and ask when someone will be in place.*

Elena: We hope to have someone in place by the end of next month.

You: *Thank Elena. Suggest a special meeting about this at ten on Monday morning.*

Elena / John / Tom: Good idea. / In my diary. / OK.

You: *Ask if there is any other business.*

Business culture

See page 107 and think about how people's expectations differ between corporate and national cultures about what should happen in meetings.

Taking the minutes and keeping control

Briefing

Taking the minutes

In a face-to-face meeting, a telephone or video-conference call, the minutes are the most important document. It is the record of the meeting and also the 'paper trail' of decisions made and action points to implement.

So what should you put in the minutes? Three things:

> WHAT? What decisions were agreed
>
> WHO? Who is responsible for implementing the action points
>
> WHEN? When the action points should be done by

Who should take the minutes?

In many meetings the chair or the convenor takes the minutes. However, if it's a big meeting, as chair you need to focus on control. Ask a member of the team to take the minutes, compile them and send them to you for checking. You should then circulate the minutes as soon as possible after the meeting. When you check the minutes of the meeting, make sure they focus on the *what*, *who* and *when* for each agenda item. Make sure they are precise.

How to keep control in the meeting

As chair of the meeting your job is to:

- establish clear objectives
- ensure information is transmitted
- manage the discussion
- keep to time
- achieve a clear and successful outcome

Establish clear objectives – make it clear in the agenda what the meeting should achieve.

Ensure information is transmitted – send out agendas, minutes, reports in good time.

Manage the discussion – make sure all views are heard and avoid personal confrontation in the meeting.

Keep to time – stop people talking for too long, avoid general conversation at the start of the meeting, make sure the meeting ends at the time agreed. If you need to go on longer, agree it with participants.

Achieve a successful outcome – summarize contributions after each speaker if necessary, summarize action points (*who* and *when* after each agenda point) and emphasize priority actions at the end of the meeting.

Listening

1 **Listen to part of a meeting where Patricia, the Chair, Karen, Nick and Barry are discussing a motorway widening project. Answer the questions.**

1   Who does the Chair ask to speak about the motorway widening project?
2   Who is surprised and angry about the 12-week delay?
3   Why didn't Karen know about the delay?
4   What is the cause of the delay?
5   What does Karen see as the main problem?
6   What does Barry suggest?
7   What does the Chair not want minuted?
8   What does the Chair want to happen?

2 **Listen again to the meeting and complete these sentences, all spoken by the Chair.**

1   Hold ...., Nick.
2   Let's .... the facts first.
3   So, let me ....
4   So what's the main problem here as you .... it?
5   I don't think that is a .... for this meeting.
6   Rather than looking to blame, let's look for ....

Business practice

1 **Listen and repeat these sentences.**

Establish clear objectives	Let's establish the facts.
	Our objective must be to get the project back on schedule.
	Let's be clear about what we want to achieve.
Keep to time	Can we keep to time? I have another meeting after this one.
	Time's moving on. Can we go on to the next item?
	We're almost out of time. Can you be brief?
Interrupt a speaker	Thanks John, you've made your point. Can we move on?
	Thank you, John. I think we've all got the point.
	We're short of time, John. Can you sum up very briefly?
Agree with a speaker	Good point, Tanya.
	I take your point, Tanya.

Ensure information is transmitted	Could you let me have me a copy of the paperwork?
	Can you send a note to remind everybody?
	Can you circulate the report you mentioned?
	Keep me up to date with developments on a daily basis.
	Can you keep everybody posted on developments?
Manage the discussion	Rather than looking to blame, let's look for solutions.
	What is the main problem as you see it?
	What are our options?
	Let's go round the table and get suggestions.
Achieve a successful outcome	Let's set up a meeting to deal with that.
	Those are all good suggestions.
	I think we've made good progress.
	We're making excellent progress.

2 Test yourself. Cover the sentences above and complete these sentences.

1 What is the problem .... you see it?

2 Let's go .... the table and get suggestions.

3 Let's look .... solutions.

4 I .... your point.

5 We're short .... time. Can you be brief?

6 Let's be .... about what we want to achieve.

3 **You are continuing to chair the meeting in 7A with your colleagues Elena, Tom and John. Follow the instructions. Then listen to the model conversation.**

You: *Ask if there is any other business. Suggest going round the table and ask Elena to speak first.*

Elena: Just one point. I'd like to raise the question of information transfer. No one told me about this meeting. I only found out about it on the general staff intranet this morning. I think that's unsatisfactory. Tom, you're responsible for communications and, frankly, you didn't communicate.

You: *Tell Elena to hold on. Ask Tom what the problem is.*

Tom: We're trying to save time and we're trying to reduce email traffic. So we decided to put the information on the intranet.

You: *Thank Tom. Ask for suggestions to make the information flow more effective.*

John: Could I make a suggestion? It's fine to put meetings information on the intranet but you need to tell us as well.

You: *Thank John for making a useful point. Ask for other suggestions.*

Elena: Yes, I can't always access the staff intranet when I'm out of the office. It's important to send me a meetings request to make sure I get it.

You: *Thank, Elena. Ask Tom to send an email to all staff to advise them about the new meetings policy. Ask him to advise key personnel by sending a meetings request.*

Tom: OK. I'll do that.

You: *Ask Tom to keep you informed about developments and to report back at the next meeting. Ask if there is any more AOB and fix the time and date of the next meeting. Thank everyone for attending.*

Business writing

Writing task

It is often useful to take your own minutes of a meeting so you can remember the important points. Think of the last meeting you attended. How much can you remember? Look at the Minutes plan below and write your own minutes for the meeting you attended.

> **MINUTES PLAN**
>
> Meeting title (title or objectives of meeting)
> Meeting date
> Meeting venue (if online, write online)
> Participants (who was at the meeting)
> Apologies (who said they couldn't attend the meeting)
> Agenda items (for each agenda item)
> * Title of agenda item
> * Action point
> * Who was responsible for action or reporting
> * When
> AOB
> Date of next meeting

Key take-aways

Write down the things you will take away from Unit 7 and how you will implement them.

Topic	Take-away	Implementation strategy – How?	Implementation time frame – When?
How to prepare an agenda			
How to run a meeting			
Meetings expectations			
How to write the minutes			

8

Participating in meetings

By the time I've thought, translated, and opened my mouth to speak, it's too late. The meeting has moved on.

— A non-native speaker talking about intervening

Aims

- How to intervene
- How to make your point
- How to interrupt and deal with interruptions
- How to adapt to different styles of participation
- How to express your opinion when speaking and writing
- How to agree and disagree in writing

A   Making your point in meetings

Quiz

How good are you at taking part in meetings? What do you think? Read the statements and choose your answers.

		Yes	No	Sometimes
1	It is hard to interrupt in a meeting when I want to speak.			
2	I find it easy to stop people interrupting me when I'm speaking.			
3	I find it easier to speak in English in meetings with other non-native speakers of English than with native speakers.			
4	It is hard to participate and make my point in meetings.			
5	It is difficult to summarize what I want to say.			
6	It is difficult to ask people to speak more slowly when I don't understand something.			
7	It is difficult to ask people to explain what they mean.			

Briefing

Many non-native speakers of English say they find it hard to make their points in meetings, especially when they are dealing with native speakers of English. So what can you do to be certain you can make the points you want to make in meetings?

How to make your points

1	Prepare	Get the meeting agenda in advance and read it. Note the points you are interested in and think about what you might want to say.
2	Tell the Chair in advance	Call or email the Chair of the meeting and make it clear that you would like to contribute on particular agenda points.
3	Sit where the Chair can see you	If it is a face-to-face meeting, sit in the eye line of the Chair so you can catch his / her eye. If you are next to the Chair or hidden by a colleague, this can be difficult. Signal to the Chair when you want to make your point, either verbally or non-verbally.
4	Make your points firmly	Use these guidelines for your intervention: **CLEAR** Be as clear as you can. Explain what you will say and why you will say it. Pause before important words and phrases so people hear them clearly. **POLITE** Always be polite. Agree before disagreeing. Respect the other person's view. **LIGHT** Don't sound too serious. When we are nervous, we often sound too serious. Breathe out before you speak. It helps lower the voice. **TIGHT** A short, clear intervention is more effective than a long one. Say what you want to say, then stop. Remember these four words: CLEAR, POLITE, LIGHT, TIGHT.

Listening

1 Listen to two extracts from a meeting about the introduction of a single business management system within a large corporation. The Chair, Don and Silvia are present. Answer these questions.

		Extract
1	In which extract does the Chair invite Don to intervene?	1 ☐ 2 ☐
2	In which extract does Don stop an interruption?	1 ☐ 2 ☐
3	In which extract does Silvia apologize?	1 ☐ 2 ☐
4	In which extract does Don make a suggestion?	1 ☐ 2 ☐
5	In which extract does Don say he has finished what he wants to say?	1 ☐ 2 ☐

40 **2** Listen again to the two extracts and complete these sentences.

Extract 1

1 The .... thing is how we manage this changeover.

2 Silvia, please can I just finish what I was .... to say?

3 Sorry, I didn't mean to be ....

Extract 2

4 John, could I .... in here?

5 I just .... to say something about technical support during the implementation phase.

6 Well, how .... if we reduced their normal responsibilities during this period?

7 That's .... I wanted to say.

Business practice

41 **1** Listen and repeat these sentences.

Ask to intervene	Could I just come in here? Could I just say something?
Make your point	I just wanted to say something about … My main point is …
Stop an interruption	Just let me finish. Hold on a moment. (*informal*)
Apologize for interrupting	Sorry. Sorry, I didn't mean to be rude.
Get back to your point	As I was saying, …
Make a suggestion	How about if we did this? Why don't we do this?
Conclude your intervention	That's all I wanted to say. That's what I think we should do.

2 Test yourself. Cover the sentences above and then complete these sentences.

1 Why .... we do this?

2 .... I was saying, we should do this first.

3 .... let me finish.

4 .... on a minute.

5 ...., I didn't mean to be rude.

6 That's all I .... to say.

3 **You are in a budget meeting and you want to make a point. Follow the instructions. Then listen to the model conversation.**

You: *Ask to intervene.*

Chair: Yes, of course. What did you want to say?

You: *Thank. Say you want to say something about budgeting for air travel.*

Sarah: But we've already discussed that!

You: *Stop Sarah's interruption and make your point – people can video-conference rather than have face-to-face meetings.*

Chair: That's a good point.

You: *Say your main point is air travel costs must come down.*

Chair: I agree with you.

You: *Say you have finished your intervention.*

Business culture

In many cultures it is natural to give your opinion, agree, disagree and challenge other people's opinions, even the Chair. In many other cultures the opposite is true.

Think of your style. Put a tick in the box if you agree with the statements. Then think of another culture you deal with. Put a tick if you think they agree too.

Statement	I agree	The other culture agrees
1 I always agree with the boss in the meeting.		
2 I am happy to challenge the boss in the meeting.		
3 If I disagree, I say so.		
4 If I disagree, I keep silent.		
5 I interrupt to say I like something.		
6 I only interrupt if I think something is wrong.		
7 I like to give my opinion in a meeting.		
8 I prefer to listen to others and not say what I think.		

Now look at the differences and think. If you are in a meeting with the other culture, should you adapt? If so, what should you do?

B   Giving your opinion

Briefing

Giving your opinion in international meetings is important. It makes people notice you and it gives you a reputation. How you give your opinion is especially important. It decides if your reputation is good or bad and if you will increase your influence or lose it.

Here are eight tips to help you give your opinion and increase your influence in international meetings.

1	Know what you want to say	Make sure you have a good reason to say something. Say it because you think it is a useful contribution to the discussion. Don't say it because you are angry or because you want to prove a point.
2	Focus on action	You want to change the way people think or what they do. Say the point you want to make simply and clearly. Focus on WHAT you want people to think or do. Then say WHY they should think or do it.
3	Be objective	Always remember there are two sides to any discussion. Don't assume your view is the only one that matters. Be prepared to recognize both sides of an argument and then state your position.
4	Focus on the problem, never the person	Don't insult, blame or complain. Be objective and fair. Focus on the facts as you see them. If you do this, more people will agree with you.
5	Don't judge	If you want to express an opinion say: 'I feel this is wrong.' Don't say: 'You are wrong.'
6	Show respect	Respect the other person even if you disagree with them. If you are wrong, be prepared to concede your point politely, never angrily.
7	Be consistent	Don't change your views or your principles. People will respect you if they know your principles and your approach. They won't respect you if you change your view all the time. However, if you do change your view, say so.
8	Be calm	A calm measured tone of voice, not too emotional or too fast, gets respect from your audience. During a conference call, be recognized by your calm, balanced tone. If you are chairing a meeting and two colleagues disagree with each other, always use a calm balanced tone of voice.

Remember: in a meeting or conference call your voice is your brand.

Listening

1 Listen to two extracts from the continuation of the meeting you listened to in 8A about the introduction of a single business management system within a large corporation. Answer these questions.

		Extract
1	In which extract does Don agree with Silvia strongly?	1 ☐ 2 ☐
2	In which extract does Don disagree with Silvia strongly?	1 ☐ 2 ☐
3	In which extract does Silvia agree with Don with reservations?	1 ☐ 2 ☐
4	In which extract does Don concede a point?	1 ☐ 2 ☐
5	In which extract does Silvia agree with Don strongly?	1 ☐ 2 ☐

2 Listen again to the two extracts and complete these sentences.

Extract 1

1 I .... agree with you.

2 Well, I agree with Don up to a ....

3 I .... your point.

Extract 2

4 Well, with all due respect to Silvia, I .... disagree.

5 What's the best way to .... this?

6 ....! We definitely need more information to work with.

Business practice

1 Listen and repeat these phrases and sentences.

How to agree strongly	Absolutely!
	I quite agree with you.
How to disagree	I agree up to a point but ...
	I understand what you're saying but ...
How to disagree strongly	With all due respect I completely disagree.
	I'm afraid I can't agree with you on that one.
How to be objective	If we look at the situation objectively, ...
	The facts of the matter are these.

How to concede	I take your point.
	In that case, I withdraw my objection.
How to manage disagreement	Let's discuss this outside the meeting.
	Can I suggest a compromise on this?
How to agree to disagree	Let's agree to differ.
	I'm afraid we have to agree to disagree on this one.

2 **Test yourself. Cover the sentences above and then complete these sentences.**

1 The facts of the .... are these.

2 I'm .... I can't agree with you on that one.

3 If we look at the situation ...., ...

4 Can we compromise .... this?

5 Let's agree to ....

3 **You are in a meeting to discuss the purchase of a new management information system. Jenny is sure which system she wants. You disagree. Follow the instructions. Then listen to the model conversation.**

Jenny: Can we all agree on the German management system?

You: *Say you have no objection to the quality but you have a strong objection to the price. Ask if Jenny can find a cheaper option.*

Jenny: No, quality comes at a price.

You: *Agree up to a point, but insist that equally good local options exist and they are cheaper.*

Jenny: Is there a cheaper option with the same quality?

You: *Explain it is important to look at the situation objectively. There are three facts to consider: quality, service and price. Ask whether Jenny has negotiated the best price.*

Jenny: Yes, I have. I don't know why you're objecting.

You: *Suggest a compromise. Get quotes on management information systems from three suppliers, local and foreign and see which is best.*

Jenny: I'm sorry, I think that's a waste of time.

You: *Say you will have to agree to differ.*

Business writing

How to agree and disagree in writing

Sometimes, you need to put your opinions in an email or memo. To write your opinions clearly and effectively, remember these points.

1 **Summary**   Write a one-sentence summary of why you are writing.

2 **Context**   Make the context clear. Say what you are writing about. Make it clear which meeting or discussion you are referring to and when it took place.

3 **Agree**   Say what you agree with first. Use phrases like:
   I agree with you about …, Although I agree with you that, …

4 **Disagree**   Now write what you disagree with and explain why you disagree. Use phrases like:
   I'm afraid I disagree with …, I strongly disagree with …, I object to …

5 **Make positive suggestions**   Write what you want to happen.

6 **Style**   Have a clear layout. Use plenty of spaces. Make it easy to read. Check it for logic and for errors and spelling mistakes. If necessary, ask a colleague to read it through.

Writing task

Look at Business practice activity 3 again. Write an email to Jenny. Summarize your opinions. Then read the model answer in the Answer key.

Key take-aways

Write down the things you will take away from Unit 8 and how you will implement them.

Topic	Take-away	Implementation strategy – How?	Implementation time frame – When?
How to intervene			
How to make your point			
How to deal with interruptions			
How to prepare a discussion paper			

9 Conference calls

Silence is golden, except in conference calls.

Aims

- How to chair and participate in a telephone conference call
- How to chair and participate in a video-conference call
- Conference call etiquette
- How to express your opinions in writing

A Taking part in telephone conference calls

Quiz

How often do you take part in telephone and video-conference calls? What are the challenges?

Read the sentences and choose Yes or No.

		Yes	No
1	I find phone conference calls more difficult than video ones.		
2	I prefer face-to-face meetings to conference calls.		
3	I find it difficult to understand people in conference calls.		
4	I'm always nervous the technology is going to break down.		
5	I prefer small group conference calls.		
6	I'm never sure when to speak in conference calls.		
7	It's difficult to interrupt in conference calls.		
8	I don't know how to disagree politely in conference calls.		
9	I think conference calls are good for information.		
10	I think conference calls are good for action.		

Briefing

Telephone conference calls pose special problems for non-native speakers. You have two main problems:

- You can't see people.
- It's difficult to identify people's voices.

Here are nine pieces of advice to overcome these two problems in order to have successful conference calls.

1 Always greet people and check who is online. Make sure you say your name clearly.

2 Always identify yourself when intervening.

3 Check you have no noisy accessories.

- Don't tap your keyboard when your microphone is on.
- Don't click your pen.
- Don't tap your fingers on the table.
- Turn off your mobile / cell phone or put it on mute.
- Take off noisy jewellery.

4 Avoid 'dead air' time. Complete silence can make people think you are offline.

5 Be careful of heavy breathing. It can sound very loud in a conference call.

6 Find ways to ask people to repeat or speak more slowly when you don't understand something.

7 If you are the Chair, find ways of asking people to speak succinctly so that you keep to time.

8 If you are the Chair, summarize contributions and at the end of the conference call summarize action points. This way you ensure there are no misunderstandings.

9 If you are the Chair, thank everyone for their participation.

Listening

1 **Listen to part of a conference call involving four people: the Chair, Bill, Jess and Nina. Tick the things that go wrong.**

Problem	
1 Speaker(s) too fast	
2 Speaker(s) too quiet	
3 Silence on line	
4 Interference on line	
5 Speaker(s) too long	
6 Speaker(s) unidentified	

2 **Listen again and complete these sentences.**

1 Please .... yourself when you intervene.

2 And also make sure you speak clearly and .... so we can all understand.

3 Keep me in the .... on that, please.

4 I think it would be good, Jess, to .... that list internally ...

5 Nina, can you .... us on progress on your project?

6 Please either press your .... button or ...

7 ... or get .... the line.

8 I think we need a contingency plan in .... things go wrong.

Business practice

1 **Listen and repeat these sentences.**

Greet people and check who is online	Let's check who is online. Bill, are you online?
	Hi, everybody. Bill here.
Identify yourself when intervening	(It's) Bill speaking.
	Jess here.
Ask people to identify themselves	Could you identify yourself, please?
	Who's speaking?
Ask people to be quiet	Please be quiet.
	Please press your mute button.
	Please stop tapping your keyboard.
Avoid 'dead air' time	Are you there?
	Yes, I'm here.
	Is Nina online?
Ask people to be slower or repeat	Sorry, could you slow down a bit, please?
	Sorry, I didn't catch that. Could you say it again, please?
Ask people to hurry up	We're running out of time.
	Could you come to your point, please?
	Could you sum up briefly, please?
Summarize action points	Thanks, just let me summarize that.
	Before we end, let me summarize the key points as I understand them.
	Let me sum up.
	To sum things up, ...
Thank everyone for participation	That's the end of the conference call.
	Thanks to everyone for participating.
	Bye for now.

2 Test yourself. Cover the sentences opposite and then complete these sentences.

1 Let me .... up.

2 We're running .... of time.

3 Sorry, I didn't .... that.

4 Could you come to your ...., please?

5 It's Sam ....

6 Thanks for ....

3 You have just joined a conference call. Think about your current project. Use PAPO (see Unit 1) and make notes about it. Introduce yourself and describe your project. Follow the instructions. Then listen to the model conversation.

Chair: Have you joined the call?

You: *Say hello, introduce yourself.*

Chair: Hi, glad you could join us. Tell us what you're working on right now.

You: *Say the title of your project and what its aim is. Describe how you are doing it and what the outcome will be.*

Chair: Great. Thank you. Let me open up to questions. No? OK. Thanks very much.

4 You are in the same conference call. This time you are the Chair. Summarize and close the call. Follow the instructions. Then listen to the model conversation.

You: *Say that time is almost up and you want to summarize the key points of the meeting. Ask if there are any questions first.*

Harry: Yes, is there a central contact point we can use if we need to get in touch?

You: *Say that you will be the central contact point and that you will circulate your contact details. Ask if there are any other questions.*

Harry: No.

You: *Summarize the key points of the meeting: Bill is getting recommendations about providers on the Brazil project in two weeks; Jess will circulate a list of suppliers they don't recommend; Nina is interviewing suppliers on the Guangzhou project; Harry is contacting sub-contractors for the Abu Dhabi airport terminal project. Check you haven't missed anything.*

Harry: No, I don't think so.

You: *Thank everybody, fix the date of the next meeting and say goodbye.*

Business culture

See page 108 for points of etiquette which you need to pay attention to during a conference call.

Taking part in video-conference calls

Briefing

Ingredients of a successful call

What are the ingredients of a successful international video-conference meeting? Let us summarize the key points here.

1	**Time**	Agree the timetable for the meeting in advance. Remember, different groups may have different ideas about punctuality and a suitable time across time zones.
2	**Hierarchy**	Find out before you start who is the most important person in the group. It may be important to address them first or with respect.
3	**Purpose**	Make sure everyone understands the purpose of the meeting.
4	**Sensitivity**	Be sensitive to different personalities when you know them. If someone is shy or uncertain, make sure they have space to speak. If someone dominates the conversation, ask them to be succinct and brief.
5	**Expectations**	If you can, find out people's expectations before the meeting in one-to-one or small group conversations. Preparing the background and knowing participants' expectations can make a big difference between a successful conference call and an unsuccessful one.
6	**Small meetings are better than big ones**	Think about having a small conference call with a few people. This may help quieter participants and non-native speakers of English. If it has to be a big meeting, you can delegate someone to summarize the discussion.
7	**Explain the context**	Always explain *why* decisions are taken, not just what the decisions are. People will feel more integrated into a strategy if they understand it, even if they don't completely agree with it.
8	**Alternative communication channels**	For people who won't speak in public, ask them their opinion in private. They may find it easier to communicate their opinions in writing.

Advice on video-conference calls

In a video-conference call there are additional problems compared with a telephone conference call, and one advantage – you can see people.

Here are five pieces of advice on video-conference calls.

1 **What's on the wall?** Anything confidential? Anything outsiders shouldn't see? Does the wall behind you promote your company? Do designs on the wall make participants look stupid?

2 **What's on the table?** Is the table tidy? Papers, coffee cups, half-eaten sandwiches? Clear the table!

3 **How are you dressed?** Bright clothes are fine. But be careful of stripes – they strobe, creating lines on the screen. Are you dressed respectably? Does your dress code match the conventions of the other people? This may particularly apply to you if you are dressed too casually or reveal more flesh than is appropriate.

4 **Can everyone see you?** Don't hide behind the large person next to you. If you are on the side, don't lean backwards, as you will be out of shot.

5 **Wave!** Six people on a video-conference call can be hard to distinguish. When you start to speak, make a gesture or wave so everyone knows who is speaking.

Listening

1 Listen to part of a video-conference call involving the same people you heard in 9A: the Chair, Bill, Jess and Nina. The Chair and Nina are together and Jess and Bill are together. Are these statements true or false?

		True	False
1	At the beginning Bill and Jess can see but not hear very well.		
2	Bill doesn't know what an SLA is.		
3	The Chair can't see Jess and Bill.		
4	The Chair says they have left the conference call.		
5	There is a problem with the video-conference call technology.		
6	They call a technician to solve their technical problem.		

2 Listen again and complete the sentences.
1 Just to ...., can you see Nina and me OK?
2 And how .... sound? Is that all right?
3 The sound's a bit ....
4 Sorry, I .... hear very well.
5 I think the satellite connection is ....
6 We .... talking about the SLAs.

Business practice

1   **Listen and repeat these sentences.**

Checking sound	Can I just check everyone can hear me OK?
	Just to check, is the sound OK?
	I just want to check the audio is clear.
Checking visuals	Just to check, can you see us OK?
	How about the video – is it all right?
	I just want to check the picture is OK.
Confirming reception	We can hear you clearly.
	We can see you fine.
	Sound is OK.
	Satellite reception is fine.
	The picture has come back up.
Reporting problems	I can't hear you very well.
	I can't see you.
	Reception is bad.
	They've gone offline.
Explaining bad reception	The sound is distorted.
	The picture quality is very poor.
	The satellite connection is down.
Referring back to before a communication breakdown	As I was saying before we were interrupted, …
	Where were we?
	Let me pick up where I left off.

2   **Test yourself. Cover the sentences above and then complete these sentences.**

1   Let me pick .... where I left off.

2   The picture quality is very ....

3   They've gone ....

4   I can't hear you very ....

5   I just want to check the audio is ....

3 You are taking part in a video-conference call with a pharmaceutical industry customer. Follow the instructions. Then listen to the model conversation.

Customer: [*distortion on line*] As you know, in clinical trials, quality standards of health and safety and careful recording of samples and results are absolutely vital to the success of the trial. Can you reassure us on those points?

You: *Apologize and say that you can't hear very well and explain why. Ask the customer to repeat what he said.*

Customer: [*distortion on line*] I said, can you reassure us about your quality standards of health and safety?

You: *Explain that you can't see or hear the customer clearly. Ask him to check the connection at his end.*

Customer: [*pause – line is now clear*] Yes, our technical adviser has just checked the system and he says the satellite reception is fine now. Can you hear and see me now?

You: *Reassure the customer that reception is fine.*

Customer: As I was saying, can you reassure us about quality standards in clinical trials?

You: *Explain that every distributor and every operator in clinical tests has two weeks' health and safety training to international standards.* [pause – picture has gone] *Say you can't see the customer but you can hear him. Ask if the satellite is down.*

Customer: We're obviously having problems with reception at our end. Thanks for your answer. It may be best to continue the conversation by email.

You: *Explain the satellite has come back up and that reception is better again.*

Customer: I think to save time it's better if we continue by email. Anyway, thanks for the reassurance on quality standards. Nice talking to you. Bye.

Business writing

See pages 108 and 109 for how to express your opinions in writing.

Key take-aways

Write down the things you will take away from Unit 9 and how you will implement them.

Topic	Take-away	Implementation strategy – How?	Implementation time frame – When?
Tips for successful telephone calls			
Tips for successful video-conference calls			
Conference call etiquette			
Ways of reporting poor reception			
Tips for successful international meetings			
How to express your opinions in writing			

10 International negotiations

You don't get what you want. You get what you negotiate.

Aims

- How to introduce yourself and your company
- How to recognize the five stages of a negotiation
- How to recognize which stage you are at
- How negotiation expectations differ across cultures
- How to write a letter of introduction

A Presenting your organization at the beginning of a negotiation

Quiz

When you start a negotiation with people you have not negotiated with before, what do you do like to do?

Read the statements and choose Yes or No, first for what is important locally and then for what is important internationally.

		Important locally	Important internationally
1	Before the negotiation I like to spend a lot of time preparing my position.	Yes / No	Yes / No
2	Before the negotiation I spend my time examining my position and also the other company's position.	Yes / No	Yes / No
3	At the start of the negotiation I like to give a bit of background to our company.	Yes / No	Yes / No
4	At the start of the negotiation I like to find out a bit about the background of the company we are negotiating with.	Yes / No	Yes / No
5	I like to get straight down to the business of negotiating.	Yes / No	Yes / No

		Important locally	Important internationally
6	I like to spend time getting to know the people I'm negotiating with before getting down to business.	Yes / No	Yes / No
7	I like to be very direct in my negotiating style and I like to bargain hard.	Yes / No	Yes / No
8	I prefer to go slowly and explore the other person's position before I reveal my own.	Yes / No	Yes / No
9	I like to make sure both sides are winners at the end of a negotiation.	Yes / No	Yes / No
10	I recognize in any negotiation there are winners and losers.	Yes / No	Yes / No

Briefing

The first thing you need to do when you begin a negotiation with a new partner, supplier or customer is to make your organization's status clear to them. Never assume that your negotiating partner knows all the relevant information about your company.

Here are eight ways you can impress the person you are negotiating with.

1	Introduce yourself	This includes explaining your own role in your organization.
2	Explain the type of company	This includes saying where your organization is based and what it does.
3	Explain the core business	This includes describing the market sector(s) and your products or services in more detail.
4	Explain the origins of the company	It is always interesting to potential partners if you give them some information about your company's history and development.
5	Explain the financial position	Without revealing any confidential information, give your negotiating partner a sense of the financial scale of your company.
6	Explain the importance	Tell your partner where you stand in comparison to the competition in your market sector(s).
7	Describe the size of the operation	Give some information about where you have branches, factories, offices and so on.
8	Describe your client base	Tell your partner about the kinds of companies and people you sell your services or products to.

Listening

1 Listen to two negotiators introducing themselves and their companies at the start of a negotiation. Which of these things do they do?

	Negotiator 1	Negotiator 2
1 Personal introduction		
2 Type of company		
3 Core business		
4 Origins		
5 Financial position		
6 Importance		
7 Size of operation		
8 Client base		

2 Listen again and complete these sentences.

Negotiator 1

1 First of all, before we get .... to the negotiations, let me tell you …

2 … let me tell you a little bit about our company by way of an ....

3 We're a family business and, in fact, the company was .... by my grandfather in the 1950s.

4 We specialize .... meat products, mainly chicken and beef.

Negotiator 2

5 To start, let me tell you a .... about the company.

6 … we moved .... wind farm technology about ten years ago.

7 Last year we .... over 150 million dollars …

8 … and this year we're looking to .... revenues by 15%.

Business practice

1 Listen and repeat these sentences.

Explain the type of company	We're a family business based in Milan. We're a multinational travel company with our headquarters in Cincinnati.

Explain the core business	We're a logistics company, specializing in supply chain management.
	We're a food processing company, specializing in meat products and a line of ready meals.
Explain the origin of the company	The company was founded by my grandfather 40 years ago.
	The corporation started in 1934 as the Electronics Company.
Explain the financial position	We have a $3 billion turnover.
	Our turnover last year was $150 million.
Explain the importance	We're the market leader in waste treatment technology.
	We're among the top five manufacturers in Spain.
Explain the size of the operation	We have branches in over 50 countries.
	We operate mainly in EMEA and the US.
Describe your client base	Our key customers are the leading supermarket chains in Europe.
	We sell to major stores all over the world.

2 Test yourself. Cover the sentences above and then complete these sentences.

1 We're .... in Dubai.

2 We .... in Africa mainly.

3 We're the market .... for this kind of software.

4 Our .... increased to £50 million last year.

5 Our main .... are large supermarkets.

6 We're a software company, ... in business software.

3 Prepare a one-minute presentation of your company for the start of a negotiation. Follow the instructions in the Briefing but note that you do not have to make the points in the same order or include every point. Make notes to help with your presentation if necessary.

4 Now present your company and, if you can, record your presentation for review. Ask a partner or colleague to listen to and comment on it.

Business culture

See page 109 to find out more about international differences between people's expectations in a negotiation.

Briefing

When you are negotiating internationally, it is crucial to have a shared understanding of what point you are at in the negotiations. It is no good if one side in the negotiations thinks they are outlining a position and the other side thinks they are reaching final agreement.

Use the five-stage approach to understand the other person's position and where they are in the negotiation.

Stage 1 Prepare

In Stage 1 each side explains their position. They explain their market needs and they say what they expect from the negotiation.

Stage 2 Explore

In Stage 2 each side discusses the other's situation. They ask questions to find out more about what the person expects.

Stage 3 Propose

In Stage 3 one or both sides makes specific initial proposals.

Stage 4 Bargain

In Stage 4 both sides bargain about what they can offer. They ask the other negotiator for concessions and they try to agree on terms.

Stage 5 Agree

This is the stage you want to arrive at. You hear a 'buying signal', a phrase that tells you the other side is ready to agree.

It sounds really simple, doesn't it? If it is simple, what's the problem? There are two:

1   You may not hear the signals.

2   The other side may change their position.

Of course, in reality, negotiations never follow the five-stage process exactly, as Stage 2 can follow Stage 1, and so on. Negotiators often raise a new point and go from the Bargain stage back to Prepare or Explore stage.

In a negotiation, your task is to recognize any stage changes and to respond to them.

Listening

1 Listen to five extracts from a negotiation. Identify the stages of the negotiation.

Negotiation	Stage
Extract 1	
Extract 2	
Extract 3	
Extract 4	
Extract 5	

2 Listen again and complete these sentences.

1 Let's .... along those lines.

2 So if we covered the costs of setting up the office in your building, you ....
   be willing to give us the space rent free … ?

3 Is this what you're ....?

4 I'm .... that we share the equity in the joint venture 60:40 in our favour.

5 First of all, let me .... our needs in general terms.

Business practice

1 Listen and repeat these sentences.

Stage 1 Prepare	The way we see things the market is expanding.
	The key issue in our market is quality product.
	The problem we face is how to source quality product at a reasonable price.
	What we want to achieve is quality, price and delivery.
	Our situation is that we are very careful about investing.
Stage 2 Explore	Tell me what you feel about the products currently on the market.
	Tell me what you think about the competition.
	On the one hand you want quality, on the other hand you want reasonable prices. Can you have both?
Stage 3 Propose	I propose we do this.
	I'm proposing we do this.
	I suggest we start small and grow the business step by step.
	Let's do this first.
	What would happen if we offered a low price but for a bulk order?
	Suppose we rebranded as our own product, would that be acceptable?
	How would you feel if we put in a trial order to test the product?

Stage 4 Bargain	If we make a large first order, will you give us a discount?
	If you agree to this, we are ready to sign an agreement.
	If you can't agree to this, we'll have to withdraw our offer.
	This is a deal-breaker for us.
	I'm not happy with that. I need to rethink.
Stage 5 Agree	I'm happy with that.
	I'm comfortable with that.
	I can live with that.
	Let's agree on that.
	I think we can proceed along these lines.

2 **Test yourself. Cover the sentences above and complete these sentences.**

1 This is a .... for us. If you can't agree, the deal is off.

2 It's not exactly what I want but I can .... with that.

3 How much .... will you give us on the price if we make a large first order?

4 If we rebranded as our own product, would that be .... ?

5 I'm happy to put in a .... order and then make a larger order if it is successful.

6 On the one hand, you want a large order. On the .... hand, you want to charge a high price. You can't have both.

7 I'm happy to lower the price if you put in a .... order for 10,000 units.

8 The .... issue in our market is quality. Quality is worth a higher price.

3 **Think about a negotiation you had or are going to have with a supplier of services or products to your company or customer. Make notes about what you might say at each stage of the negotiation.**

4 **Now record what you want to say at each stage. Ask a partner or colleague to listen to and comment on it.**

Stage 1 Prepare
Outline your general position.

Stage 2 Explore
Find out about your partner's position.

Stage 3 Propose
Make initial proposals.

Stage 4 Bargain
Focus on the details of the proposal.

Stage 5 Agree
Agree terms.

Business writing

A letter of introduction

How do you introduce yourself to a potential new customer by letter or by email? Read the letter of introduction on page 110 and answer these questions.

1   What is the reason for the letter?

2   What kind of company does the supplier represent?

3   What can the company offer the customer?

4   What is the supplier's track record?

5   What are the next steps?

Writing task

Now imagine a situation in your own business. You have to write your own letter of introduction. Draft the letter.

Key take-aways

Write down the things you will take away from Unit 10 and how you will implement them.

Topic	Take-away	Implementation strategy – how?	Implementation time frame – when?
How to introduce yourself and your company			
The five stages of negotiation			
Language of the five negotiation stages			
How negotiation expectations differ across cultures			
How to write a letter of introduction			

11 Negotiation styles

Never cut what you can untie. — Joseph Joubert

Aims

- How to present your position
- How to prepare and explore
- How to propose and bargain
- How negotiation styles differ
- How to update or ask for advice in writing

A

Preparing and exploring

Quiz

At the preparing and exploring stage of a negotiation what are your preferences? Read the statements and choose Yes or No.

		Yes	No
1	I prefer to state my objectives at the beginning of the negotiation.		
2	I prefer to wait until I have heard the other person's objectives before stating mine.		
3	I think it's important to explain my own objectives.		
4	I think it's important to question the other person's objectives first.		
5	I like to show I'm open to compromise early in the negotiation.		
6	Once I have stated my objectives, I refuse to compromise.		
7	I find it easy to understand the progress of a negotiation in my language.		
8	I find it difficult to understand the progress of a negotiation in another language.		

Briefing

At the PREPARE and EXPLORE stages of a negotiation, which we introduced in 10B, you present your position. Before you do this it is very important to know four things.

1 **Know what you *want* to have** They include your 'must-haves' and a few 'give-aways' that you can offer if you need to.

2 **What you *must* have** These are your minimum requirements. You need these for the negotiation to be successful.

3 **Your BATNA** This is your BEST ALTERNATIVE TO A NEGOTIATED AGREEMENT. In other words, if you can't get what you want, your BATNA is your second best option.

4 **Your 'walk-away' point** This is the point where you have to stop negotiating. It is similar to your minimum requirements.

At the PREPARE stage you do three things:

1 You agree the procedures of the negotiation.

2 You explain your objectives.

3 You explain your market and the opportunities you see.

And you ask your partner to do the same.

At the EXPLORE stage you do three things:

1 You question your partner.

2 You ask for clarification of things you don't understand.

3 You check you have understood your partner's position correctly.

In the PREPARE stage, remember these three points:

1 Establish rapport.

2 Agree the agenda.

3 Say in general terms what you want to achieve. Ask what the other side wants to achieve.

The EXPLORE stage in a negotiation is about asking questions and clarifying the other side's position. It has three important aims:

1 It creates a dialogue.

2 It helps you find out about the other negotiator's preferences.

3 It helps you find out their priorities, and their entry points and exit points.

The *entry point* is the start of a negotiation. The *exit point* is the point where the other side stops negotiating, the 'walk-away' point.

The two key skills you need in the EXPLORE stage are:

• how to listen

• how to ask questions

Listening

1 Listen to a negotiation between two company representatives, Nick and Donna. Donna represents a company that is supplying products to Nick's company. Answer these questions.

1 Who states the key points for negotiation?

2 How many key points are there for negotiation?

3 What is the first point for negotiation?

4 What is the second point for negotiation?

5 Who suggests they move on to the second point for negotiation?

2 Listen again and complete these sentences.

1 So, let's kick ....

2 Let's .... the agenda first.

3 And how do you want to ....?

4 .... I start?

5 So could you say a .... more about that?

6 What we'd like to .... is a win–win situation for our customers ...

Business practice

1 Listen and repeat these sentences.

Fix the agenda	Let's start by agreeing the main points we want to cover.
	What are the main points you want to raise?
Agree a procedure	How do you want to proceed?
State your aims	What we want to achieve is a win–win solution.
	My aim is to clarify the situation so we can see the way forward and plan the next steps.
Listen positively	That's interesting.
	Yes, please go on.
Use questions	Could you say a little more about that?
	If I understand correctly, you are concerned about on-time delivery. Is that right?
Summarize	So what you are saying is ...
	So let me summarize what we've agreed.

2 **Test yourself. Cover the sentences opposite and then complete these sentences.**

1 What are the main points you want to ....?

2 We want to achieve a .... situation.

3 Can I .... the situation?

4 Can we plan the next ....?

5 If I understand ...., you are concerned about quality.

6 So let me summarize what we have ....

3 **You are at the beginning of a negotiation. You sell a high-priced luxury product. A supplier wants you to sell a range of products at different prices. Follow the instructions. Then listen to the model conversation.**

You: *Welcome the other negotiator, suggest you start the negotiation and agree the agenda.*

Negotiator: That's fine with me. Those are the points I wanted to cover.

You: *Ask what procedure the other negotiator would like to follow.*

Negotiator: Well, if it's OK with you, let's both state our positions and then we can start to discuss them.

You: *Agree. Suggest the other negotiator starts.*

Negotiator: Well, as I see it, the main issue we need to address is price. We need a range of cheaper products.

You: *Check you have understood correctly. Does the other negotiator want to expand your catalogue with cheaper products?*

Negotiator: Basically, yes. I think it will create a far more attractive sales proposition for you.

You: *Explain that your organization has built up a loyal clientele through word-of-mouth recommendations because you have a reputation for high quality and they are prepared to pay a premium price.*

Negotiator: So what you're saying is high quality, high price is good.

You: *Agree. Say the market for luxury products is still expanding so you don't see a need to change strategy at this stage.*

Negotiator: And you don't think the situation will change?

You: *Say that's not what you meant. Explain that if the market changes you might consider new product ranges and a different pricing strategy. But not yet.*

Negotiator: OK. So let's move on to point two on the agenda.

Business culture

See page 111 and think about the key factors that influence how decisions are made.

Proposing and bargaining

Briefing

The **PROPOSE** and **BARGAIN** stages follow the **PREPARE** and **EXPLORE** stages.

Proposing

When you propose, you make an offer to the other negotiator.

RULE 1 Make your initial proposals on the basis of what you agreed in the EXPLORE stage.

RULE 2 Allow the other side to make counter-proposals.

RULE 3 Sell the benefits of the proposal to the other side.

RULE 4 Explain the benefits of the proposal for you.

Bargaining

When you bargain, you discuss with the other negotiator to find the best solution for both of you. In a street market this often means finding the lowest acceptable price. This process is called *haggling*. **Bargaining depends on conditions. 'If you do this, we will do this.' And there are rules for successful bargaining.**

RULE 1 Always make an offer with a condition.

RULE 2 Never give something for nothing.

RULE 3 If you don't like the condition, propose a counter-bargain.

RULE 4 Don't argue, question.

RULE 5 Always confirm what you have agreed before you address issues you don't agree on.

And remember: nothing is agreed until everything is agreed – make agreements provisional until the end of the negotiation.

Listening

1 Listen to a negotiation between Caroline, the supplier, and Pete, the customer. Answer the questions.

1 Who makes which proposal?

Proposal	Caroline	Pete
1 Trial order of 1,000 units at list price and on sale or return		
2 Trial order of 500 units at list price and on sale or return		
3 Trial order of 1,000 units at 25% discount		

2 Which proposal is agreed?

3 These are the negotiating points. Which ones is Pete flexible on? Which ones is he inflexible on?

Point	Flexible	Inflexible
1 Product volume		
2 Price		
3 Delivery		
4 A no-questions-asked refund		
5 Payment terms		

2 Listen again and complete these sentences.

1 Would you be prepared to make a .... order?

2 It would be a good way to .... the market.

3 In .... we could consider that.

4 We could offer you 1,000 units at .... price.

5 What would you .... if we offered you a 25% discount ...?

6 Do we have any .... on delivery?

7 All our contracts are signed on one basis, 90 days' payment. We would .... to do that with you.

8 I'm afraid that is ....

Business practice

1 Listen and repeat these sentences.

Make a proposal	Let me make a proposal. I suggest we do this. I propose we do this.
Invite counter-proposals	How do you respond to this? What do you think of this proposal? How do you feel about this?
Sell the benefits	This will help you maximize your business. This will give you a higher profile in your market. This is a very good offer.
Explain the benefits to you	The advantages from our point of view are ... This relationship will help our company achieve a higher market profile. Working together will enhance our profitability.
No offer without condition	If you can agree to this, I can offer you a discount. If you could manage this, I could agree that. If I ordered a million units, what discount would you offer?

Never give something for nothing	I will offer this provided you agree to that.
	I will do this as long as you keep to our agreement.
	I will agree to this provided we can complete within the agreed time frame.
Propose a counter-bargain	Could I suggest an alternative proposal?
	Could I suggest we approach this from another angle?
	Let me make a counter-proposal.
Don't argue, question	Can you explain why you feel that?
	Please explain to me once more how you arrived at that figure.
	Can you tell me how you reached that decision?
Always confirm agreements	Let's summarize what we agree so far.
	Let me recap on what we've agreed.
	Before we discuss outstanding issues, let's confirm what we've agreed.

2   **Test yourself. Cover the sentences above and then complete these sentences.**

1   How do you .... about this?

2   Let me .... on what we've agreed.

3   I will do this as .... as you keep to our agreement.

4   I will agree to this .... we can complete within the agreed time frame.

5   Working together will .... our profitability.

6   If I ordered 500,000 units, what discount would you ....?

3   **You are in a negotiation. Respond to the other person's proposals and offers. Follow the instructions. Then listen to the model conversation.**

You: *Summarize what you've agreed: 1,000 units at 15% discount; immediate delivery; 90 days' payment terms.*

Negotiator: That's right.

You: *State you have offered a no-questions-asked refund policy for delays and delivery. Client asked for a customer helpline.*

Negotiator: That's right.

You: *Say the helpline is a development cost normally passed to the client. Propose to pay for development but request 30 days' payment terms.*

Negotiator: This is difficult for us. These are our standard terms and conditions.

You: *Say again you will incur extra costs and need to recover costs quickly. Suggest 60 days' payment terms.*

Negotiator: We've already agreed to take 1,000 units at 15%. If we agree to 60 days' payment terms, will you agree to 20% discount?

You: *Suggest splitting the discount at 17.5%.*

Negotiator: I suppose that's possible. OK.

You: *Summarize the agreement again: 1,000 units at 17.5% discount; 60 days' payment terms; a helpline for customers.*

Negotiator: I'll need to check my figures with our finance department but I think we can proceed along these lines.

Business writing

See page 112 for information on how to update colleagues and ask for advice, and read the email there before you do the Writing task.

Writing task

Now imagine this situation. You are reporting to Alex in Dublin. You are providing security for an international exhibition. You have been contracted to provide 300 security personnel. You have hired and trained 250 local staff but you are short of 50 personnel.

Your solution is to hire 50 foreign personnel to complete the contract. However, this will mean higher pay, transport and accommodation costs. The alternative is penalty charges for failure to complete the contract as agreed.

You need Alex to approve your proposal. How can you compose your email to get him to agree to your proposal? Write your email and then compare it with the model answer in the Answer key.

Key take-aways

Write down the things you will take away from Unit 11 and how you will implement them.

Topic	Take-away	Implementation strategy – How?	Implementation time frame – When?
How to present your position in a negotiation			
Preparing and exploring			
Proposing and bargaining			
How negotiating styles differ			
How to update colleagues and ask for advice in writing			

12 Closing the negotiation

Always give the other guy his bus fare home. — Anon

Aims
- The language of closure
- How to deal with 'difficult' customers
- How to deal with last-minute problems
- How to write a letter of intent

A Reaching agreement

Quiz

Which of these statements do you agree with?

1 If I can't get an agreement, I will walk away from the negotiations.

2 If I can't get an agreement, I will put the negotiation on hold and reconsider my position.

3 If I don't like the attitude or approach of the negotiator, I am less likely to make concessions to reach agreement.

4 If I trust the negotiator personally, I am usually prepared to make concessions to reach agreement.

5 I think it's important to celebrate an agreement with a small gift.

6 I think it's important to celebrate an agreement with a meal or, at least, something to drink.

7 If business conditions change, I expect my partners to be flexible regarding the agreement.

8 Once a contract is signed we honour it, whatever happens.

9 If I make a mistake in the terms of the agreement, I expect the other side to renegotiate on that point.

10 When a contract is signed we can't change any details.

Briefing

The last stage of the negotiation process is AGREEING. This is what we call the CLOSE.

Agreeing can be very difficult, especially if the person you are negotiating with is not cooperative. How do you deal with 'difficult' negotiators? At the end of a negotiation, if you have not reached an agreement, you have three alternatives:

- **Concede** – agree to demands made by the other side.
- **Compromise** – make small concessions and hope for concessions from the other side.
- **Walk away** – withdraw from the negotiation.

To help reach agreement, you may use these strategies:

1 Propose concessions that are acceptable to all sides.

2 Agree to 'split the difference' (agree to move to a central agreed position) between both sides.

3 Offer two or three alternatives.

4 Introduce new proposals or incentives.

5 If there is a stalemate, have an adjournment.

Here are the things you should do at the AGREE stage:

1 **Record any agreements.**
   Make sure everything is recorded to avoid misunderstandings or disagreement.

2 **Don't ignore detail.**
   If it isn't in the agreement, it may not be done.

3 **Be confident but not aggressive.**
   If you are concluding a negotiation, always be supportive of the other person. They may be your partner for a long time.

4 **Make sure that the people in the negotiation have the authority to conclude the negotiation.**
   Check the sign-off procedure on both sides. Make sure it corresponds to when you intend to start work.

> **Glossary**
>
> **Stalemate** is a situation in which neither side in an argument or contest can win or in which no progress is possible.
>
> An **adjournment** is a temporary stopping of a trial, enquiry or other meeting.

Listening

1 Listen to part of a negotiation where the outstanding issue is cost. Annie and Karl use five techniques to try and reach agreement. Which techniques are successful and which are unsuccessful in this case?

Strategy	Successful	Unsuccessful
1 Propose a concession		
2 Agree to split the difference		
3 Offer two alternatives		
4 Introduce a new idea		
5 Take a break and reconvene		

2 **Listen again and complete these sentences.**

1 Shall we .... what we've agreed?

2 .... not, I'm afraid.

3 .... we agree to split the difference?

4 Well, as I see it, we have two ....

5 Let me make another ....

6 Let's take a .... and think about it ...

Business practice

1 **Listen and repeat these sentences.**

Record any agreements	Let's note what we've agreed so far. What are the main points that we've agreed? Shall we check what we've agreed?
Check anything that isn't clear	I'm sorry I'm not clear about … Could you just explain what you mean by …? I just need to clarify one or two things …
Review alternatives	As I see it, there are two alternatives. An alternative might be to … I can see no alternative to this course of action.
Introduce a new idea	One way to resolve this problem is to … Let me make another suggestion. Could I suggest a way of resolving this situation? Suppose we agree to split the difference.
Check detail	Can I just check some details? Could you clarify that? Could you explain what you mean? Just so we're clear …
Be positive	I'm sure we can come to a successful agreement. We're nearly there. All we need to do now is agree this. Let's take a break and think about it.
Agreeing	I think we have a deal. We agree to go ahead. That's a deal then.

2 **Test yourself. Cover the sentences opposite and then complete these sentences.**

1 I'm sure we can come to a successful ....
2 Can I just .... some details?
3 Let's .... what we've agreed so far.
4 We're .... there.
5 Could I suggest a way of .... this problem?
6 We .... a deal.

3 **You are close to agreement at the end of a negotiation. Follow the instructions. Then listen to the model conversation.**

Negotiator: OK, so we've agreed on specification, price and quantity.

You: *Agree.*

Negotiator: There's just the issue of delivery dates.

You: *Ask the person to clarify what they mean.*

Negotiator: Well, we haven't fixed dates yet.

You: *Agree with what the person says. Suggest the end of March for delivery of the units.*

Negotiator: I don't think we can manage that.

You: *Suggest an alternative: half in mid-March and half in mid-April.*

Negotiator: That might be possible. I'll have to ask my board.

You: *Be positive.*

Negotiator: I agree. We're nearly there.

Business culture

Closing a negotiation can be tense, especially if time is short and the other person is being 'difficult'. When things are not going well, we often go back to our own natural way of doing things. Think about a difficult negotiation. Answer these questions.

1 Did you decide the other person was impolite?
2 Did you make hostile remarks to the other person?
3 Did you stop smiling? Did your voice become hard?
4 Did your behaviour become more formal or more aggressive?
5 Did you decline the offer of hospitality, for example dinner or a social event?

These are common reactions when you deal with a 'difficult' negotiator. Remember these positive actions:

- Try to understand their point of view.
- Pause the negotiation and take a break to give yourself time to think.
- Take the opportunity to talk to negotiators informally during breaks and dinners.

Think of a difficult negotiation. Did you try these strategies? What was the result?

B Dealing with last-minute problems

Briefing

At the end of a negotiation you have reached agreement in principle. What do you do if a problem arises? How do you deal with it? There are a number of solutions. If you wish to look for a compromise, there are a number of things you can do:

- Emphasize the benefits of the collaboration.
- Encourage and applaud any constructive proposal by the other side.
- Say that you are looking for a solution that is acceptable to both sides.
- Give the other side an escape route, a way to avoid any difficulty.

Above all, don't allow a last-minute problem in the negotiation to affect your attitude. Be polite and positive at all times. Try these tactics:

- Praise the other side.
- Emphasize mutual benefit.
- Emphasize common ground.
- Remain polite but persistent.
- Ask why the other side has a problem.
- Agree on a date to review concessions.
- If the other side walks out, contact them IMMEDIATELY.
- Agree a date for future talks.

Listening

1 Listen to Gina calling Bob about a last-minute problem in the takeover of Bob's company. There are two phone calls. Answer these questions.

1 What is the problem?

2 How does Gina propose to resolve it?

3 What is the outcome of the first phone call?

4 Which solution to the problem does Bob choose in the second phone call?

2 Listen again and complete these sentences.

1 I'm calling because I'm afraid we have a ....

2 What .... of a problem is there?

3 What will happen if we can't .... this problem out?

4 If we can't sort this out, then we may have to call .... the deal.

5 So how can we .... the situation?

6 I'm sure we can work this ....

7 I said I'd get .... to you on the accounts problem.

8 Well, in principle, ... that there are no more problems with ...

Business practice

1 **Listen and repeat these sentences.**

Signal there is a problem	I'm calling because we have a problem. I'm sorry to say there is a problem. I'm afraid we have a hitch.
Ask about the problem	What kind of problem is there? What exactly is the problem? What's the hitch?
Ask about outcomes	What will happen if we can't sort this problem out? If we can't agree on this, what happens then? What would be the result if we couldn't deal with this problem?
Speculate on outcomes	If we can't sort this out, then we may have to call off the deal. If we sorted this problem out quickly, then the deal could go ahead. If you can't deliver on time, we'll have to introduce penalties.
Remain positive	I'm sure we can sort this out. Don't worry. We can fix this, I'm certain.

2 **Test yourself. Cover the sentences above and then complete these sentences.**

1 If we can't sort this ...., then the deal can't go ahead.

2 What .... is the problem?

3 I'm sorry to .... there is a hitch.

4 Don't .... I'm sure we can fix this.

5 What .... be the result if we couldn't deal with this problem?

6 I'm .... because there's a problem.

🎧 **3** **A company you are signing a contract with calls you to tell you there is a problem regarding US rights. Follow the instructions. Then listen to the model conversation.**

68

Negotiator: Hi there. I'm calling because we have a problem.

You: *Ask what the problem is.*

Negotiator: We're preparing the contract now and I think we're making really good progress but we have a problem on exclusivity. Let me explain. We want world rights but we don't have rights to the US.

You: *Explain you agreed to give rights to the rest of the world but you want to keep US rights.*

Negotiator: Our problem is that the US is our biggest market. We need US rights to deliver the revenues to meet the contractual payments to you. This is a deal-breaker for us. If we can't agree on this we may have to withdraw from the agreement.

You: *Emphasize the benefits of the deal. Stress that you are looking for a win–win agreement. Ask if it's possible to meet halfway.*

Negotiator: Possibly. I think it's important we reach an agreement. What do you propose?

You: *Propose to license US rights as a separate agreement, provided you get a higher proportion of revenues from US sales.*

Negotiator: Let me be sure I understand correctly. You will give us rest of world rights as agreed and you will give us US exclusivity under a separate agreement but you want a higher proportion of the US revenue. Is that right?

You: *Confirm this and say you think it would help resolve the problem.*

Negotiator: OK. That's a positive proposal. I'll put it to the board. Thanks for your cooperation on this. I appreciate it. I'll get back to you as soon as possible.

Business writing

At the end of a negotiation, before you sign an agreement it is common to write a letter of intent. This is not a legal document. It explains what each partner intends to do, when and at what price. A letter of intent is often the basis for the contract.

Writing task

1 Read the model letter of intent opposite. Then think of a negotiation you have been involved with. Draft a letter of intent to your negotiating partner. Include what you will do, when and at what price.

Dear _____ ,

LETTER OF INTENT
I would like to confirm our intent to conclude an agreement with you for the (*service or product*) subject to contract.

ACTION
We agree that you will (*action*).
On our side we will (*action*).

TIME
We intend to begin the agreement on (*date*) and complete by (*date*).

BUDGET
The agreement will offer a fee of (*amount*) payable in (*currency*) and an agreement about shared costs. The total budget for the project is estimated at (*amount*) with a contingency of (*amount*).

DUE DILIGENCE
The agreement will be subject to a due diligence examination of each side's organizational and financial resource allocation.

NEXT STEPS
Agree contract.
Appoint project manager.
Finalize project workflow and milestones.

2 Think about one of your past negotiations. Write a letter of intent on the basis of what you agreed.

Key take-aways

Write down the things you will take away from Unit 12 and how you will implement them.

Topic	Take-away	Implementation strategy – How?	Implementation time frame – when?
Language of closure			
Dealing with difficult customers			
Language for reaching agreement			
Techniques for dealing with problems			
How to write a letter of intent			

Business file

This section provides you with additional reference material for the Business culture and Business writing parts in some of the units.

 2A Active listening – the key to networking

Business culture

Look at the questionnaire and tick the descriptions that match your style.

Style	
Eye contact	
1 I prefer to look people in the eye when I talk to them.	
2 I prefer to avoid direct eye contact. I think it is disrespectful.	
3 I look people in the eye but then I look away quickly. I don't want to seem aggressive.	
4 I worry that people who don't make direct eye contact are not honest. They are trying to hide something.	
Silence – Some cultures are known as 'silent' cultures. They dislike interruptions and prefer to take time to reflect and think before they reply.	
5 I am uncomfortable with silence. If someone is silent, I prefer to say something.	
6 I am comfortable with silence. If there is a silence in the conversation, I don't need to break it by talking.	
7 I like to pause and reflect before I answer what someone else says.	
8 I hate it when people interrupt.	
9 I don't mind when people interrupt. That is normal conversation, isn't it? It shows they are interested.	
10 If people are silent, I don't know what they are thinking. I can't trust them.	
Body language – The way you use your hands, the way you stand or sit and how close you are to other people are all part of your body language.	
11 When I talk I use my hands to emphasize what I say.	
12 When I talk I use a lot of gestures with my hands and arms.	
13 When I am with people I stand or sit up straight.	
14 When I am with people I am very relaxed. If I am sitting down I lean back in my chair.	
15 When I am sitting down I often cross my legs.	
16 When I am sitting down I sometimes cross my legs and put one ankle on my knee.	
17 When I talk to someone I prefer to be close to them.	
18 When I talk to someone I prefer to stay at least one arm's distance apart.	

Now think about another nationality you deal with. Are they the same or different? If they are different, why do you think that is? Do you need to adapt your style?

2B | ## Using F.A.C.E.

Business writing

Writing task

Read this email and then rewrite it. Use phrases from the table on page 22 to make it more polite and friendly.

To:	David
From:	Liz
Subject:	New project

David,

I got your email.
Send me some more information about the new project.

Liz

Liz Spellman
Production Manager
Failsafe Maintenance Ltd

3A | ## How to start a conversation

Business culture

Look at this list of topics. Which ones are *ice-breakers* or *ice-makers* for you? Add notes to the table.

Topic	Ice-breaker	Ice-maker
Partners and families		
National politics		
Business trends		
National culture		
National success		
National heroes		
Religion		
Sport		
Wealth		
Property and possessions		

Think of someone from another country that you deal with. Which topics might be ice-breakers or ice-makers for them?

Business culture

Generally speaking, what do people expect from a presentation? Think about what *you* expect. Is it one of these things? Tick the boxes for *Me* or write in the 'Something else' box.

	Facts and details	Benefits to you	Empathy and good feelings	A product or service you can buy, use or invest in	Something else
Me					
Someone else					

Now think of another country, region, organization or company department you work with. What do they expect? Write in the table for *Someone else*.

Do you need to adapt your style if you are presenting to these people? How will you adapt? Complete this sentence: *I will be more / less ...*

How to prepare

Business culture

What do people in different parts of the world expect from a presentation? Here are six common challenges you might face.

Serious or funny?	In some cultures it is important to be serious in your presentation and not to make jokes or tell funny stories to get the audience's attention. In other cultures the audience expects to be entertained and amused, as well as informed or persuaded. If you have an international audience for your presentation, be very careful about introducing humour or trying to entertain your audience. Jokes often do not travel well across cultures. Interesting stories or anecdotes – especially those from your own personal experience – may be a better way to get the audience on your side and interested in what you have to say.
Long or short?	Timing is important. People's attention span is shorter than you think, especially if they have to listen in a foreign language. However, your audience may expect you to give a lengthy presentation to justify their attendance.
Facts or ideas?	Some audiences may expect a lot of information – statistics and suchlike. Others may want ideas and to know what you think. They prefer to read the detailed information in handouts and on a website later.

What to do when the technology goes wrong?	What do you do when something goes wrong? Imagine the projector doesn't work or you can't find your notes! Many presenters can get the audience to sympathize with them if they have problems. However, be careful. If you are not in control of your technology, it may look unprofessional. Sometimes you can make a joke of a problem but not too often.
Applause or silence?	Some audiences, if they like what they have heard and appreciate the effort you have made, like to applaud. However, people may applaud in different ways. In most countries they clap their hands but in some countries, for example, they knock on the table. This can be a bit of a surprise for presenters who don't expect this sort of reaction.
Questions or no questions?	As we saw in 4A, you may accept questions in the middle or at the end of your presentations. But some cultures may prefer not to ask any questions in public. Always be prepared to leave a short time for people to come up to you afterwards with their questions.

Setting the agenda

Business culture

People from different corporate and national cultures have differing expectations of what should happen in meetings. What are your expectations? Tick your answers A or B.

1A	I expect decisions and actions.	**1B**	I expect to find out what other people think. The decisions are taken outside the meeting.
2A	I expect to receive instructions.	**2B**	I expect people to consult me.
3A	I expect to receive information.	**3B**	I expect people to ask my opinion.
4A	I expect to focus on positive aspects and solutions.	**4B**	I expect to focus on problems. It's more realistic.
5A	If I have a good idea, I like to discuss it in the meeting.	**5B**	I think meetings are for confirming what we have discussed and agreed before.
6A	I prefer to talk about 'we' in meetings. The team is most important.	**6B**	I think it's important to talk about ourselves in meetings. The individual is most important.
7A	In a meeting I like to share my ideas on any subject on the agenda.	**7B**	In a meeting I prefer to discuss items within my area of responsibility.

Summarize your style by writing the letters A or B in the boxes below.

1	2	3	4	5	6	7

Now think of another colleague or manager (maybe from another culture) who has a different style from you. Write the letters that describe their style.

1	2	3	4	5	6	7

How can you adapt to work more successfully with them in meetings?

9A Taking part in telephone conference calls

Business culture

During a conference call you need to pay attention to these points of etiquette:

Respect   If you don't know the other people on a conference call, ask how they would like you to address them. They may wish to be more formal than you expect. Be prepared to use family names and titles. If talking to British, American and Australian particpants, for example, be prepared to use first names immediately.

Levels of politeness   Some people may avoid any criticism or confrontation and be extremely polite, even if they disagree with you. Others may be very direct. This difference, when people don't understand or don't know, can cause problems in communication in both phone and video-conference calls.

Use of silence   Some people believe it is important to stay silent and reflect before answering. Others dislike silence and, when there is a period of silence, their natural reaction is to jump in and say something to fill the gap. Check before the conference call if the person is likely to prefer silence and pauses before replying. Be prepared to wait and give them time to reflect before they speak.

Leaders talk, others stay silent   In some groups only the leader answers questions and junior people are expected to be quiet unless they are specifically asked to speak by the group leader. Be sensitive to this. Find out who is the leader of the group at the other end of the conference call. Address questions and comments to them first.

Think of your style. What do you prefer? Then think of a group or person you deal with in conference calls. Is their style the same as yours or different? How might you need to adapt?

9B Taking part in video-conference calls

Business writing

How to express your opinions in writing

Sometimes you may want to express your opinions in writing before or after a conference call rather than speaking during the conference call.

Read the example opposite. Andrew didn't want to speak at the meeting but wants to make sure his views are represented. He emails Katie, the Chair, after the meeting.

When expressing opinions, keep to a maximum of five bullet points and make sure your writing is brief and to the point.

Remember these three things:

- Always start with POSITIVE points.
- Leave NEGATIVE points till later.
- Always have a conclusion (advice or recommendations).

Writing task

Think of a meeting you can't attend but you want to tell people what you think. Summarize your thoughts. Use the principles and format presented opposite.

Dear Katie,

In this morning's meeting I didn't want to speak but I would like to make these points about the proposal.

- It's a positive idea to use materials from outside sources. This will save time.
- It's also good to reuse material in a different situation for the same reason.
- However, we must be careful to make sure that we have permission to use and adapt the material.
- It may be quicker and safer to produce our own material rather than reuse other people's.
- Also it means the material will be our intellectual property and not shared.

In conclusion, I think, on balance, we should produce our own original material.

Regards,

Andrew

 Presenting your organization

Business culture

What are people's expectations in a negotiation? People from different cultures do not always have the same expectations of a negotiation.

Here are some of the key international differences. Identify your style and then compare it with another culture you deal with. Put a tick in the boxes that are closest to your personal style.

Hard sell I want them to sell me the product and tell me how good it is.		**Soft sell** I want them to tell me the product's qualities and disadvantages. I want to make up my own mind.	
Company pride My key concern is to support my company.		**Personal career** My key concern is to develop my personal career.	
Risk embracing I calculate risks but I am prepared to take them when necessary.		**Risk averse** If there is a risk, I prefer to avoid it. I am careful to obey the rules and never go outside them.	
Close I like to stay close to my customer. I telephone and visit them when I can.		**Distant** I prefer a distant relationship by email through official channels.	
Positive orientation I believe that you should always emphasize the positive, look for opportunities and be optimistic.		**Negative orientation** I believe you should focus on problems, find out what went wrong and improve it. It is better to be realistic than always optimistic.	

Now think of an international partner, client or supplier you deal with. What are they like? How should you adapt to their style of negotiation?

Business writing

Read this letter and answer the questions on page 87.

Dear _____ ,

Congratulations on your joint venture with Abu Dhabi Airport construction authority. I notice that you will be responsible for supplying aircraft hangars and terminal buildings and I believe my company may be able to help.

We are manufacturers and suppliers of high-grade industrial paint. It is specially prepared paint which is designed to look good and resist wear and tear for a period of two years before any repainting is needed.

We are a family company based in the UK with our own manufacturing plant and we have been in business since 1987 and have supplied high-grade industrial paint to construction projects all over the world.

We have supplied paint to the Lantau Island airport construction project in Hong Kong, Terminal 5 at Heathrow Airport in the UK and railway terminal projects, such as Birmingham New Street station in the UK as well as the 2012 London Games Olympic Stadium.

Our service includes producing industrial paint to your technical specification, in the colours you require and delivery to your construction site, all at a reasonable price.

If you are looking for a contractor to provide paint supplies, we would be delighted to assist. I attach details of our services. As a first step, perhaps I could call you on receipt of this letter to discuss your requirements.

Yours sincerely,
James Thompson

Sales Director
Industrial Paints

Preparing and exploring

Business culture

Eight key factors influence how decisions are made. If you understand your partner's decision-making process, it will help you negotiate agreements. Decide your style first. Then compare your style with a person you negotiate with.

Style	My style	Other person's style
1 **Individual** I take my own decisions on my own budget and responsibility.		
2 **Team** I always discuss with my team and I implement the agreed team decision.		
3 **Time tight** For me time is very important. I don't like wasting time in long negotiations.		
4 **Time loose** For me it is important to get every detail right. This takes time. I don't mind long negotiations.		
5 **Top down** Decisions come from the top. I can negotiate the best position I can but someone else must agree it.		
6 **Delegation** If I go into a negotiation, I make sure I have the authority to agree the final terms.		
7 **Facts** I make a decision based on facts and figures. Personalities are not important.		
8 **Instinct** Instinct is important. I must like and trust my partner.		

How might you have to adapt your negotiating style to work well with your partners?

11B Proposing and bargaining

Business writing

How to update colleagues and ask for advice

Francelle's manager in Delhi is Dilip. Francelle needs advice on a negotiation. She sends an email to Dilip. Here is her email. Notice how she structures it.

Greeting (*informal*)	**To: Dilip**
	Subject: Product negotiation
Topic summary	Hi Dilip,
Give the positive information	Here is an update on the product negotiation.
	The client is happy to take 500 units as a trial order. They will advertise the product on their website as a premium star buy. They insist on delivery immediately following order. They insist on 90 days' payment terms. This is non-negotiable.
Give new proposal	I have offered them 1,000 units at 17.5% discount. They want us to organize a customer service helpline to deal with delivery enquiries.
Give reasons	I think this will give us a higher initial market profile.
Get approval	Is it OK to go ahead on this basis?
Sign off	Regards, Francelle

Answer key

Unit 1 Introductions

1A How to introduce yourself

Quiz
You should usually give this information: name, nationality, job title, company, company location, purpose of visit.

Listening

1

	Name	Nationality	Job	Company	Location	Pitch
Speaker 1	✓	✓	✓	✓	✓	
Speaker 2	✓	✓	✓	✓		✓
Speaker 3	✓	✓	✓	✓	✓	✓
Speaker 4	✓	✓		✓	✓	✓
Speaker 5		✓	✓	✓	✓	✓
Speaker 6	✓		✓	✓	✓	✓
Speaker 7	✓	✓	✓		✓	

Speaker 3 gives the complete answer.

2

1 False. Jim is a production manager.
2 False. Tony works for a supermarket chain.
3 False. Marianne is based in Toronto.
4 True.
5 True.
6 False. Jean works in Wisconsin (in the USA) and wants to learn about Europe.
7 False. Azim is from Kerala but is based in Mumbai.

Business practice

2

1 for	5 here
2 May	6 responsible
3 based / located	7 based / located
4 from	8 introduce

1B How to describe your current project

Listening

1

Current project 1
P energy generation
A predict world energy needs in the next 25 years
P questionnaires and interviews
O a report in December

Current project 2
P a bid
A a nuclear power station in France
P planning and costing with partners
O submit the bid by the end of the year

Current project 3
P source new customers
A increase customer base for new products
P Identify key customers and make appointments to meet them
O ten new large customers by the end of this year

Current project 4
P prepare monthly figures
A calculate gross margin for the month just ended
P contact partners, collect figures, check them, complete the report
O a higher gross margin

2

1 pretty tight	3 at the moment
2 have to	4 objective

Business practice

2

1 outcome	4 purpose	7 contractor
2 agreement	5 supplier	8 overseas
3 responsible	6 based	

3

1 in	3 for	5 in
2 for	4 on	6 on

Unit 2 Listening

2A Active listening – the key to networking

Listening

1
1   active listener   3   non-listener
2   pretend listener   4   marginal listener

2
1   Oh, dear!   4   Kate says nothing.
2   Really?   5   He takes a phone call.
3   Maria sounds worried.

Business practice

See the Model conversation in the Audio script.

3

See the Model conversation in the Audio script.

2B Using F.A.C.E.

Listening

1
1   Clarifying
2   Empathizing
3   Focusing (He says nothing except *Uh huh*.)
4   Acknowledging

2
1   He asks a question.   3   Only *Uh huh*.
2   He sounds excited.   4   I see. I'm with you.

Business practice

2

See the Model conversation in the Audio script.

Business writing
Possible answer
Hi David,
Thanks for your email.
Nice to hear from you. It's a long time since we've been in contact.
Could you send me some more information about the new project?
Thanks and regards,
Liz

Liz Spellman
Production Manager
Failsafe Maintenance Ltd

Unit 3 Small talk

3A How to start a conversation

Listening

1
1   Social experience   4   Professional
2   Personal experience   experience
3   National experience   5   Regional experience

2
1   Was that interesting?
2   Have you been there before?
3   How often do you get back there?

4   And where were you before?
5   And when did it all change?

Business practice

2

1   mind   3   long   5   Have
2   special   4   before   6   to / from

3

See the Model conversation in the Audio script.

3B How to avoid causing offence

Listening

1

Sonia crosses these cultural fault lines:
3 Regional differences
4 Political differences
5 Differences in economic status
6 Differences in the status of men and women

2

1 Her question: 'Do you mind if I ask you another question?' This demonstrates that she knew she was about to ask a sensitive question. At the end she said, 'Interesting, thank you.'

2 She was not diplomatic enough in her first three questions. She was more diplomatic in her fourth question.

3 The delegate was very diplomatic. He responded positively but neutrally to all her questions.

4 He ended the conversation politely by offering to get her another drink, which suggests he wanted to finish the conversation.

Business practice

2

1 Would	3 mind	5 problem
2 Do	4 sorry	6 subject

3

See the Model conversation in the Audio script.

Business writing

1

1 An invitation to his host's home for a meal.
2 He may have caused offence by asking about his host's wife and family.
3 It is normal to ask about partners and families.
4 He thinks it may not be normal to ask about partners and families in his host's country.
5 He says he is sorry he may have said the wrong thing.
6 He wants to see his host again and entertain him.

Unit 4 Presentation organization

4A How to structure your presentation

Listening

1

See the Audio script: the **Three Ss** are shown in bold.

2

1 going	3 point	5 listening
2 interrupt	4 made	6 happy

Business practice

2

1 answer
2 conclusion
3 last
4 entitled
5 would
6 If

4B How to deal with questions and interruptions

Listening

Question 1
Thank ✓
Repeat ✓
Answer ✓
Check ✓
Refer to team or website ✗
Offer to contact questioner ✗

Question 2
Thank ✗
Repeat ✓
Answer ✗
Check ✗
Refer to team or website ✗
Offer to contact questioner ✓

2

1 She says: 'Please, let me just finish.'

2 He says: 'I have another question.'

3 She says: 'If I understand correctly … '

4 She says: 'Well, I'm afraid I don't have the answer to that question.'

Business practice

2

1	understood	4	refer
2	afraid	5	team
3	back	6	deal

3

See the Model conversation in the Audio script.

Unit 5 Preparation and delivery

5A How to prepare

Listening

1

1 Key message: we have to manage our energy resources or experience a major change in our way of life.

2 Main points: need to conserve energy resources better; need to develop new forms of energy to meet future needs; managing and developing energy resources is crucial at economic, social and personal levels.

5B Joint presentations

Listening

1

1 Presentation style: lively. Kirsten and Sue have good voice projection and lively intonation, and they sound enthusiastic.

2 They sound as if they work together; they mention each other's names; they say 'We' and not 'I'; they thank each other; they sound like a team.

3 Introduction to the new site: Kirsten
Details of what you can do on the new site: Kirsten and Sue
How you can put content on the new site: Kirsten

4 By previewing a new feature which she expects the audience to be positive about.

Business writing

1 The main points: research, training and training materials.

2 There is a paragraph for each main point.

3 The conclusion says why the question is important and summarizes the most important recommendations.

4 The report is clear because: the title is clear; the summary makes the three main points; each main point has its own paragraph; the conclusion summarizes the main points and the recommendations.

3 The challenge of energy resources affects everyone.

4 He asks the audience to imagine a world without energy.

5 He refers back to the previously mentioned role of his company.

2

1	imagine	4	say
2	how	5	crucial
3	thing	6	coming

2

1	love	4	back
2	Over	5	forward
3	hand		

Business practice

2

1	back / over	3	joint
2	yours	4	Let

3

See the Model conversation in the Audio script.

Unit 6 Presentation style

6A Presentation delivery techniques

Listening

The tour operator uses all six techniques.

2

1	Ask a question	4	Make a contrast
2	Group points in threes	5	Repeat for emphasis
3	Sell an experience	6	Just one more thing

Ask a question: 'How many of you have taken a holiday in Croatia yourselves?'

Group points in threes: 'Well, there are three things you can be sure of when you holiday in Croatia: culture, history and the good life.'

Sell an experience: 'So, let me take you on a journey. You arrive at the airport. A taxi takes you along the beautiful coast with the gleaming Adriatic below you, past the medieval walled city and through the pine trees to your hotel overlooking the sea.'

Make a contrast: 'But remember, you don't just come for sun. You also come for culture and history and fun!'

Repeat for emphasis: 'So let me repeat it one more time. Come to Croatia. Croatia is culture. Croatia is history. Croatia is the good life.'

Just one more thing: 'Oh, and one more thing. Remember to bring your swimming costume. The water is wonderfully warm at this time of the year.'

Business practice

2

1 Make a contrast
2 Groups points in threes
3 Just one more thing
4 Sell an experience
5 Repeat key messages
6 Ask a rhetorical question

6B Voice and visuals

Listening

1

Stresses important information ✓
Uses silence ✓
Varies speed ✓
Varies volume ✓
Pauses for effect ✓
Refers to the slide ✓
Repeats what is on the slide ✗

2

1	main	3	shows	5	intend
2	look	4	point		

Unit 7 Running a successful meeting

7A Setting the agenda

Listening

1 Where to hold event: Landmark Hotel
2 Who to invite: 20 staff (+ 1)
3 Budget for event: £60 per head
   (£50 + £10 X 21 = £1,260)
4 Inviting a special guest: The chairman

AOB 1 Tony is on leave from Friday week – all expenses to him by start of next week

AOB 2 Frances says there is a problem with the post service – need an earlier collection time

Date of next meeting: July 6th 10 a.m.

2

1	coming	4	other
2	apologies	5	agreed
3	minutes		

Business practice

2

1	take	4	send
2	round	5	arising
3	kick		

3

See the Model conversation in the Audio script.

7B Taking the minutes and keeping control

Listening

1

1 Karen

2 Nick

3 The joint venture partners did not inform her.

4 A failure to complete the paperwork because local authority permissions were late coming through.

5 They do not control the schedule.

6 Meeting the joint venture project manager, Gilberto, and offering him support with the paperwork.

7 The discussion

8 Karen should talk to Gilberto weekly and keep the Chair informed on developments.

2

1	on	3	summarize	5	matter
2	establish	4	see	6	solutions

Business practice

2

1	as	3	for	5	of
2	round	4	take	6	clear

3

See the Model conversation in the Audio script.

Unit 8 Participating in meetings

8A Making your point in meetings

Listening

1

1	Extract 1	3	Extract 1	5	Extract 2
2	Extract 1	4	Extract 2		

2

1	key	3	rude	5	wanted	7	all
2	going	4	come	6	about		

Business practice

2

1	don't	3	Just	5	Sorry
2	As	4	Hold	6	wanted

3

See the Model conversation in the Audio script.

8B Giving your opinion

Listening

1

1	Extract 1	3	Extract 1	5	Extract 2
2	Extract 2	4	Extract 1		

2

1	quite	3	take	5	resolve
2	point	4	completely	6	Absolutely

Business practice

2

1	matter	3	objectively	5	differ / disagree
2	afraid	4	on		

3

See the Model conversation in the Audio script.

Business writing

Model answer

Dear Jenny,

MIS meeting

I am writing to say that I'm afraid I disagree with you about the German MIS you proposed in our meeting today.

Although I agree with you that the quality and service of the German MIS are good I have a strong objection to the price.

The reason is we can get a better price from local suppliers. Even if we buy the German system we should negotiate a lower price.

I suggest we put the project out to tender and get three quotes from local and foreign suppliers. That will give us excellent quality and service but also a lower price.

Regards,

Unit 9 Conference calls

9A Taking part in telephone conference calls

Listening

1

1   Speaker(s) too fast ✓
2   Speaker(s) too quiet ✗
3   Silence on line ✓
4   Interference on line ✓
5   Speaker(s) too long ✓
6   Speaker(s) unidentified ✓

2

1	identify	4	copy	7	off
2	concisely	5	update	8	case
3	loop	6	mute		

Business practice

2

1	sum	4	point
2	out	5	speaking
3	catch	6	participating

3

See the Model conversation in the Audio script.

4

See the Model conversation in the Audio script.

9B Taking part in video-conference calls

Listening

1

1	True	3	True	5	True
2	False	4	False	6	False

2

1	check	3	distorted	5	down
2	about	4	couldn't	6	were

Business practice

2

1	up	3	offline	5	clear / OK / good
2	poor / bad	4	well		

3

See the Model conversation in the Audio script.

Unit 10 International negotiations

10A Presenting your organization at the beginning of a negotiation

Listening

1

1   Personal introduction: 1 Yes; 2 No
2   Type of company: 1 Yes; 2 Yes
3   Core business: 1 Yes; 2 Yes
4   Origins: 1 Yes; 2 Yes
5   Financial position: 1 No; 2 Yes
6   Importance: 1 No; 2 Yes
7   Size of operation: 1 Yes; 2 Yes
8   Client base: 1 Yes; 2 Yes

2

1	down	4	in	7	turned
2	introduction	5	bit	8	increase
3	founded	6	into		

Business practice

2

1   based
2   operate
3   leader
4   turnover
5   customers
6   specializing

10B The five stages of a negotiation

Listening

1

Extract 1: Agree
Extract 2: Bargain
Extract 3: Explore
Extract 4: Propose
Extract 5: Prepare

2

1	proceed	**3**	saying	**5**	outline
2	would	**4**	suggesting		

Business practice

2

1	deal-breaker	**3**	discount
2	live	**4**	acceptable

5	trial	**7**	bulk
6	other	**8**	key

Business writing

1 The letter is exploring the opportunity to supply industrial paint to a new international construction project.

2 The supplier represents a family company that manufactures high-quality industrial paint.

3 The company manufactures and delivers high-grade industrial paint to client specifications.

4 The supplier has a strong track record in supplying international airport and rail construction projects.

5 The supplier wants the client to discuss requirements and suggests a phone conversation to initiate discussions.

Unit 11 Negotiation styles

11A Preparing and exploring

Listening

1

1	Nick	**3**	Product specification
2	Four: product specification, price, delivery, next steps	**4**	Price
		5	Donna

2

1	off	**3**	proceed	**5**	bit
2	agree	**4**	Shall	**6**	achieve

Business practice

2

1	cover	**4**	steps
2	win–win	**5**	correctly
3	clarify	**6**	agreed

3

See the Model conversation in the Audio script.

11B Proposing and bargaining

Listening

1

1

1 Trial order of 1,000 units at list price and on sale or return: Caroline

2 Trial order of 500 units at list price and on sale or return: Pete

3 Trial order of 1,000 units at 25% discount: Caroline

2

Proposal 3 is agreed: trial order of 1,000 units at 25% discount

3

1 Product volume: Flexible
2 Price: Flexible
3 Delivery: Inflexible
4 A no-questions-asked refund: Inflexible
5 Payment terms: Inflexible

2

1	trial	**5**	say
2	test	**6**	flexibility
3	principle	**7**	expect
4	list	**8**	non-negotiable

Business practice

2

1	feel	**3**	long	**5**	enhance
2	recap	**4**	provided	**6**	offer

3

See the Model conversation in the Audio script.

Business writing

Model email

Hi Alex,

I'm writing with an update on the Expo security contract. As you know, we are contracted to provide 300 security personnel.

We have hired 250 local personnel. We have trained them and they are ready for Expo. However, we need 50 more personnel to complete the contract.

My proposal is to bring in 50 trained staff from other countries. This will mean we complete the contract on time and cut training costs. It will also mean we avoid possible penalty charges for non-completion.

However, we will have to pay higher salaries and incur travel and accommodation costs.

Financially, the project will cost more but less than penalty charges would cost us.

Is it OK to go ahead on this basis?

Let me know soonest.

Regards,

Unit 12 Closing the negotiation

12A Reaching agreement

Listening

1

1 Propose a concession: Unsuccessful
2 Agree to split the difference: Unsuccessful
3 Offer two alternatives: Unsuccessful
4 Introduce a new idea: Successful
5 Take a break: Successful

2

1	check	**3**	Suppose	**5**	suggestion
2	Absolutely	**4**	alternatives	**6**	break

Business practice

2

1	agreement	**3**	note	**5**	resolving
2	clarify / check	**4**	nearly	**6**	have

3

See the Model conversation in the Audio script.

12B Dealing with last-minute problems

Listening

1

1 That due diligence has shown a discrepancy on Bob's company's accounts. The company is paying off a loan from the bank, which Gina did not know about.

2 By lowering the offer price or by asking Bob to pay off the loan and interest before the deal is completed.

3 Bob is going to consider his options and talk to his finance people.

4 To pay off the loan and interest now (by taking out a personal bridging loan to cover the period between now and the contract signature and payment).

2

1	problem	**4**	off	**7**	back
2	kind	**5**	resolve	**8**	provided
3	sort	**6**	out		

Business practice

2

1	out	**3**	say	**5**	would
2	exactly	**4**	worry	**6**	calling

3

See the Model conversation in the Audio script.

Audio scripts

Unit 1   Introductions

Track 01

1   Hi, I'm Jim. I'm from Australia. I'm production manager for Transpetroleum. We're in Western Australia, in Perth. Pleased to meet you.

2   Hello, I'm Tony from China. I work for a large supermarket chain and I'm the purchasing manager. I'm here to find some new suppliers.

3   We didn't say hello. I'm Marianne from Toronto in Canada. I'm a lawyer and I work for a large international law firm. Our head office is in London but I'm based in Toronto. So I'm just here to see what's new.

4   Can I introduce myself? My name's Mary McLaughlan. I'm Scottish. I work for Mountain Energy. We're based in Edinburgh. I want to find out more about the oil and gas business.

5   Hello, I'm from Germany. I'm General Manager in Pappenheimer. We're a large organization based in Stuttgart and I'm here because I'm interested in developments in the industry. Here's my card.

6   Good morning, my name's Jean Kent. I'm President of Milwaukee Associates. We're based in Wisconsin and my interest here is to understand more about what is going on here in Europe.

7   Hi, I'm Azim Battacharya. I'm from Kerala in the south of India but I work in Mumbai. I'm a company accountant. So, what do you do?

Track 02

See the sentences in 1A.

Track 03

See the text in 1A.

Track 04

Current project 1
The focus of my current project is energy generation. Its aim is to predict world energy needs in the next 25 years. I'm sending questionnaires to major energy corporations and also interviewing industry leaders and government ministers in ten leading oil and gas producers. The outcome will be a report to be published this December. So the schedule is pretty tight.

Current project 2
The project I'm working on right now is putting together a bid for a tender for a new nuclear power station in France. We have three partners, two of them are French, and we are doing the planning and costing. We have to submit the bid by the end of the year.

Current project 3
My main project at the moment is to source new customers. We need to increase our customer base for our new products. I'm identifying key customers in the EU and making appointments to meet all of them. The outcome? Ten new large customers by the end of this year.

Current project 4

My main task right at this moment is to prepare the monthly figures. The objective is to check revenue and costs and to calculate the gross margin for the month just ended. To do that I have to contact all our partners in the UK and in the Netherlands and in Brazil to collect the figures. Then I have to check them and complete the report. The outcome, I hope, will be a higher gross margin.

Track 05

See the sentences in 1B.

Track 06

See the sentences in 1B.

Unit 2　Listening

Track 07

Conversation 1

A: Hi, Paula.

B: Hi there. How's the project going, Nicky?

A: Not very well, Paula, I'm afraid.

B: Oh, dear. Sorry to hear that.

A: Yes, we're overbudget and late.

B: Really? Do you want a fix a time and sit down and talk it through?

A: That would be great. Could I check my diary first and fix a time for a meeting?

B: Of course. Don't worry about it. I'm sure we can get back on track.

A: I'll email you.

Conversation 2

A: You know, Steve, I'm not sure about this new regional sales manager.

B: What's the problem, Maria?

A: He's not meeting his monthly sales targets.

B: Let me have a look at the figures.

A: I'll email them to you. Thanks. I'm very worried I made the wrong choice.

B: Let me look at the figures first and then we can decide what to do.

Conversation 3

A: Did you hear the good news, Kate?

B: No, what happened, Tom?

A: We got the Chinese airport contract.

B: Oh, I've got some good news for you. I think we're going to get the chance to tender for that bridge-building contract in Brazil. I've been working on that for six months.

Conversation 4

A: So why are you attending this exhibition, Mr Klein?

B: We have a stand and we're launching some new software.

A: Sounds interesting.

B: Yes, it is. Excuse me, I need to take this call. [*pause*] Right.

A: I was saying it sounded interesting.

Track 08

See the sentences in 2A.

Track 09

Model conversation

Nicky: Hi there.

You: *Hi, Nicky. How's the project going?*

Nicky: Not very well, I'm afraid.

You: *I'm sorry to hear that.*

Nicky: Yes, we're over budget and late.

You: *No! Really?*

Nicky: Yes, I'm a bit surprised too.

You: *I'm sure we can fix this.*

Nicky: That would be great. Could I check my diary and fix a time for a meeting?

You: *Don't worry. It'll be OK.*

Track 10

Model conversation

Sam: Hello.

You: *Hi, how's it going?*

Sam: I wanted to ring and tell you. I got the promotion!

You: *No! Really?*

Sam: Yes. I start next month.

You: *Great! Congratulations! Well done!*

Sam: Thanks. It's going to be hard work.

You: *Well, if you need any help, let me know.*

Sam: Thanks, I'll remember that.

Track 11

Conversation 1

A: So those are our three types of heating element and our customers are in white goods, as I said, the automotive industry and also in the airline industry.

B: And which type of heating element is most popular?

A: In our industry currently it's tubular heating.

Conversation 2

A: I'm responsible for the technical side of things.

B: That's great!

A: Thank you. But I'm also responsible for the costs.

B: That's really interesting.

A: Yes, I have to calculate the turnover on each product, the costs, the gross margin. Then I have to calculate the shared costs with head office for administration and licence fees and work out the EBIT. That's earnings before income tax.

B: That's great.

Conversation 3
A: We're a German company with manufacturing facilities in ten countries around the world. We provide heating elements to the white goods industry and to the automotive industry. White goods is dishwashers and washing machines and fridges.

B: Uh huh.

Conversation 4
A: We manufacture three types of heating element – tubular heating, radiant heating and induction heating.

B: I see. I'm with you.

A: We use tubular heating in ovens and grills. We use radiant heating in ovens under glass and induction heating in fridges.

B: That's interesting.

Track 12

See the sentences in 2B.

Track 13

Model conversation

Tim: Have you heard the good news?

You: *No, I haven't. What is it?*

Tim: We got the Canada contract.

You: *I see. That's terrific. When did you hear?*

Tim: Well, we got an email confirming the deal last night.

You: *An email? Who from?*

Tim: The email was from the government.

You: *Well done.*

Tim: Thanks. We must find a way to celebrate.

You: *Yes, you're right. We must.*

Unit 3   Small talk

Track 14

Conversation 1
A: What did you do before you took over this department?

B: I worked in Logistics.

A: Was that interesting?

B: It was OK. But Production is much more exciting.

Conversation 2
A: Do you have any holiday booked for this summer?

B: Yes, in fact I just made a booking to go to Morocco.

A: Wow! Have you been there before?

B: Yup, I went hiking in the Atlas Mountains a few years ago but this time we're going to surf on the Atlantic coast.

A: Sounds good.

Conversation 3

A: Do you mind my asking where you are from? I can't place your accent.

B: Not at all. I'm from the Philippines.

A: The Philippines. How often do you get back there?

B: Not enough.

Conversation 4

A: How long have you worked in this company?

B: Nearly ten years, I'm afraid.

A: And where were you before?

B: Oh, in an entirely different business. You won't have heard of them.

A: Oh, OK.

Conversation 5

A: So tell about the area around here. What should I know?

B: Well, it's very industrialized now, as you saw on the way in from the airport.

A: And when did it all change?

B: About 50 years ago. Before that it was very agricultural. Mainly dairy farming.

A: Really. A bit different now.

Track 15

See the sentences in 3A.

Track 16

Model conversation

You: *Where are you from?*

Colleague: I'm British. From Scotland, actually.

You: *Oh, really? What part?*

Colleague: I'm from Aberdeen. It's in the east of Scotland.

You: *And what's special about it?*

Colleague: Oh, it's the oil capital of Scotland. It's the centre of oil and gas drilling in the North Sea. I'm working there now.

You: *How interesting! And what did you do before this job?*

Colleague: Oh, before that I was at university in Edinburgh. I taught engineering.

You: *How was it different?*

Colleague: Well, I was teaching students. Mainly Scottish. Now I'm working with oil and gas engineers from all over the world – especially from the US.

You: *Have you travelled a lot?*

Colleague: Yes, a lot. Too much really. I was in Mexico last week and Indonesia the week before. It's exhausting.

Track 17

Sonia: Not many women here, are there?!

Delegate: Yes, that's because this is an official occasion and partners are not invited.

Sonia:	Oh, I see. You're from round here, are you?
Delegate:	No, I'm from the North East.
Sonia:	Oh, that's the poorer part of the country, isn't it?
Delegate:	Well, it's an economic regeneration zone and there is a lot of investment there. Personal GDP has risen by fifteen per cent in the last five years.
Sonia:	Oh, I see. Do you mind if I ask you another question? I've heard there's a lot of tension between the North East and the capital. Is that true?
Delegate:	There was once, many years ago. The North East wanted independence. But with the economic regeneration zones the North East recognizes the value of being part of this country. The government investment programme in the regions is working and that comes from the capital.
Sonia:	Interesting, thank you.
Delegate:	May I get you another drink?
Sonia:	Oh, yes, please. Thank you.
Delegate:	Excuse me, just a moment.

Track 18

See the sentences in 3B.

Track 19

Model conversation

You:	*John, do you mind if I ask you about the political situation here?*
John:	Feel free. What would you like to know?
You:	*Well, is it true that the President's brother is a paid consultant to your company?*
John:	Ah, I'd rather not discuss that if you don't mind.
You:	*OK. I'm sorry if I said the wrong thing.*
John:	Don't worry about it.
You:	*Would you mind if I asked another question?*
John:	Go on.
You:	*Where are we having dinner tonight?*
John:	That's much easier to answer!

Unit 4   Presentation organization

Track 20

Speaker: I'm going to talk about the international migration of labour. My presentation will last about five minutes and I will make three main points. The first is why migration is a problem, the second is an EU research project for dealing with the problem, and third, how you can access information about the EU project. **If you have any questions, please feel free to interrupt.**

My first point is why migration is a problem. Because of climate change and economic difficulties, migration into EU countries is expected to rise in the next 20 years. For example, the populations of countries like Great Britain, with a population of 60 million, are likely to rise by up to 20 million to 80 million by 2050. This will mean many foreign new workers joining companies and organizations and this will cause tension between local workers and new workers. This will partly be political because of pressure on jobs but it will also be cultural because of different expectations of the workplace, and in working relationships and differences in the way we work. So the population will expand. This will put pressure on the workplace and create problems in building good relations. It will be a real crisis if we don't handle it well. **That was my first point.**

My second point is to introduce a new EU project for dealing with this. The EU has tried to anticipate the problems of mass labour migration, in particular from the poorer countries in the East and South to the richer economies of the North and North West. In 2007 the EU sponsored a ten-country research project into potential problems caused by labour migration in six industries. They called the project Diverse Europe at Work. They published the research in two forms, first as country reports for each of the ten countries involved, and secondly as sector reports on each of the industry sectors across all ten countries. The industry sectors studied were transport, hospitality, manufacturing, education, retail and healthcare, all industries that employ a lot of migrant labour. As a result of this research, the EU team identified a series of 16 issues that cause tension in day-to-day host country and migrant labour relations. As a result of the project, they sponsored a set of video and print materials to help migrant workers and local workers build good relations. So the EU has gone some way to anticipate the problems, research and identify solutions and commission video and print materials for training and facilitation. **That was my second point.**

My third point is to explain how you can access the EU project. You can access the project by visiting www.dew-net.eu. There are three access points. First, you can access the country and sector research documents, compiled by each country team. Secondly, you can access the video and print support sample materials, designed for use by learning and development personnel but also by self-help groups and teams in the workplace. Thirdly and finally, there is a train-the-trainer course of one week, sponsored by the EU under the Grundtvig and Leonardo Lifelong Learning Programme.

So the work itself, the materials and training in how to use them can all be made available. **That was my third point.**

I have made three points. First, I described the problem of international labour migration, second, I described a new training project to help migrant and local workers work together better, and finally, I gave you the Web address so you can visit the project. That's my presentation. **Thank you for listening. If there are any questions, I'll be happy to answer them.**

Track 21

See the sentences in 4A.

Track 22

Questioner:	Excuse me, I have a question.
Presenter:	Of course. Go on.
Questioner:	I'm not sure that it's possible to harmonize relations between workers of different nationalities. How can you really do that?
Presenter:	Thank you for the question. The question was, how can you harmonize relations between workers of different nationalities?
	The answer is that we look at typical problems that arise at work and we discuss them from each person's point of view.
Questioner:	[*interrupts*] But doesn't that make things worse?
Presenter:	Please, just let me finish. As they discuss the differences, they begin to understand each other's points of view and they also see the similarities between them. So actually it's a very good way of building good relationships between people from different backgrounds. Does that answer your question?
Questioner:	I think so. I have another question.
Presenter:	Yes?
Questioner:	How many nationalities have worked in your company in the last five years and how long on average have they worked for you?
Presenter:	If I understand correctly, you want to know how many nationalities we have and how long they've worked for us. Well, I'm afraid I don't have the answer to that question to hand, but give me your business card after the presentation and I'll get back to you. Would that be OK?
Questioner:	That's fine. Thank you.

Track 23

See the sentences in 4B.

Track 24

Model conversation

You:	*Right, that's my presentation. Are there any questions?*
Questioner:	Yes, I have a question about costs. How can you be sure you can keep to budget?
You:	*Thanks for your question. You asked how we can be sure we can keep to budget. Well, we've spent a lot of time on the figures and I'm confident they are accurate. Does that answer your question?*
Questioner:	Well, I'm not convinced. I think you'll go over budget.
You:	*Well, I can make the detailed figures available to you later, if you like.*
Questioner:	Thanks. That would be very useful. I have another question.
You:	*And what's your question?*
Questioner:	What happens if you do go over budget?
You:	*I'm confident that won't happen. Does that answer your question?*
Questioner:	Yes, thanks.

Unit 5   Preparation and delivery

Track 25

Speaker: Good morning, everybody. What I want to do in this presentation is set before you the main challenge we face in the twenty-first century. We have to manage and develop our energy resources much better than we are doing now or experience a radical change in the way we live and a significant reduction in our quality of life.

Can you imagine a world without energy? Without electric light, heating and air conditioning, hot running water, TVs and computers? Well, it's possible if we don't meet this challenge.

So how do we manage and develop our energy resources better?

Well, the first thing we have to do is to conserve our energy resources better. How many of you have got your laptops still switched on while I speak? Yes, quite a few of you. Well, we've got to find ways to be more energy efficient and to reduce unnecessary energy consumption.

The second thing I want to say is we have to develop new forms of energy that will meet future needs, not only in the developed world but in developing countries where demand is expected to soar in the next ten years. And this is where our company comes in.

The third point I want to make is that managing and developing energy resources is crucial at three levels: economically, socially and personally. So today, I'm talking to you not just as colleagues in the energy industry but as consumers of energy.

So, coming back to where our company comes in, what I want to focus on now in the rest of the presentation is what we can offer in terms of developing new energy resources.

Track 26

See the sentences in 5A.

Track 27

Kirsten:	Good afternoon, everyone. I think most of you know me, I'm Kirsten Lang and I'm Communications Manager for the company. And this is my colleague, Sue Brown.

Sue:	Hi, everyone.
Kirsten:	So what we're going to do this afternoon is present our brand new staff intranet. There's a special new feature on it which I know you're going to love. We'll only take a few minutes of your time. I'll introduce it and then Sue will tell you about this wonderful new feature. OK? So the new intranet has all the information you need to know about the company and about day-to-day operations. For example, you can use it to contact people in different departments and to learn about the status of our projects. But it also has a special section called Staff news. Over to you, Sue.
Sue:	Thanks, Kirsten. Yes, Staff news is a really important initiative. Why? Because it's all about you. It's a way for all of us to keep in touch and find out what we're all doing. So, if you've got a piece of news – maybe you've won the lottery, had a baby or got married or you've found a wonderful place for a holiday – let us know. We want to hear your personal news and also – and this is very important – your ideas about how the company works and suggestions for how we could improve things. OK? To find out how to use the new site, let me hand you back to Kirsten. Kirsten – back to you again. It's all yours.
Kirsten:	Thanks, Sue. Well, we said we'd tell you how to send news about yourselves and suggestions for improvements to the way we do things. It's simple. All you have to do is send us an email with your news, ideas and suggestions, and we'll put them on the intranet. Or you can call me on my extension 1224. This is going to be really exciting and a lot of fun, so do give us a call. Thanks a lot and we'll look forward to hearing from you as soon as possible. Any questions …?

Track 28

See the sentences in 5B.

Track 29

Model conversation

You:	*Hello, everyone. The purpose of this presentation is to tell you about the new training programme. This is Tomas Schmidt, who will be presenting with me.*
Tomas:	Good morning, everyone.
You:	*I will introduce the programme and then Tomas will go into the details.*
Tomas:	Yes, I'll give the details afterwards.
You:	*So, let me introduce the programme. The idea behind it is to increase productivity at the same time as improving job satisfaction. Believe it or not, we really want people to enjoy what they do more!* [pause] *So, over to you, Tomas.*
Tomas:	Thank you. Here are the details. The programme will be modular and will run over a period of 12 months. In liaison with your line manager, you choose the parts of the course that are best for you. There are ten and you must do at least five. The parts cover things like Working in teams and Time management. OK, so back to you.
You:	*Thanks, Tomas. What I'd like to do now is look in more detail at the reasons for the programme. Have a look at this slide. It shows …*

Unit 6   Presentation style

Track 30

Speaker: Let me start with a question. How many of you have taken a holiday in Croatia yourselves? OK, not many of you, I see.

Well, there are three things you can be sure of when you holiday in Croatia: culture, history and the good life.

So, let me take you on a journey. You arrive at the airport. A taxi takes you along the beautiful coast with the gleaming Adriatic below you, past the medieval walled city and through the pine trees to your hotel overlooking the sea.

But remember, you don't just come for sun. You also come for culture and history and fun! And that's what you find in our beautiful city of Dubrovnik.

So let me repeat it one more time. Come to Croatia. Croatia is culture. Croatia is history. Croatia is the good life.

Oh, and one more thing. Remember to bring your swimming costume. The water is wonderfully warm at this time of the year.

Track 31

See the sentences in 6A.

Track 32

Speaker: I want to talk today about the company's plans to make video-conferencing the main way we have international meetings. Now we do recognize that there are times when you just have to meet face-to-face, so don't worry. We're not banning air travel to meet colleagues, just asking you to consider whether it is really necessary. And I know we've all had rather frustrating experiences with video-conferencing, with technical problems and so on, and that many of us find them more stressful than face-to-face meetings. But against this, we have to think of the cost of air fares to the company.

Have a look at this slide on costs. Quite staggering figures really! We must get this cost down. Let's have a look at another slide. This shows total employee hours in the air. Now I know a lot of you work when you're on a flight but what if we added time spent at immigration or going through security?

So my main point is this. The amount of air travel is not an efficient use of our resources or our time. And this is where a better use of video-conferencing comes in.

What we intend to do is two things. Firstly, use the best video-conferencing technology available and employ expert staff to run it. Secondly, ensure everyone who has to use it is well trained and supported whenever they have to video-conference. Let's have a look at the roll-out for this plan ...

Track 33

See the sentences in 6B.

Unit 7   Running a successful meeting

Track 34

Chair: Hi, thank you for coming. It's a short meeting today. George sends his apologies. He's away. Everyone else is here. Can someone take the minutes, please?

Amy: I will.

Chair: Thanks, Amy. You all got the minutes of the last meeting, right? Good. And any matters arising? None? Good. So let's take the minutes as read. Let's go through the agenda items. We've only got one really, the staff party, which is going to be a dinner on a Friday in a month's time. Amy, you were going to provide some suggestions.

Amy: Well, we had various possibilities but we decided the Landmark Hotel had a private dining room and offered good value so we'd like to suggest that.

Chair: Good thinking, Amy. Any other comments? Good. The Landmark. Now, the big question, who should we invite? Staff only, or partners and clients as well? What are your thoughts on that?

Tony: I think staff only. It's a good chance to get together and talk. If we invite clients and partners, it won't be such a useful event.

Chair: OK. Any other thoughts on that? Frances?

Frances: Yeah. I know the Chairman will be in town that week for a conference. If he was free to come along and meet everybody and give an after-dinner speech, I think it would be a real plus.

Chair:	Good idea. Everyone agreed then? Right. I'll invite him. So we've missed out the most important item – budget. Tony?
Tony:	Amy and I checked the budget and for 20 staff plus an invited guest we can do it for £50 a head. So that's £1,050 in total but the hotel can also provide a reception before the meal and they're prepared to do that for a special price of £10 a head. That's good value. So if we do both we can get away with under £1,300.
Chair:	Thanks, Tony. Happy with that. So let me summarize. We'll coordinate with the Chairman who's in town that week. I'll invite him. Amy, you'll confirm with the Landmark for the meal and the reception for 21 people, just staff and the Chairman. OK. Good, so let's go round the table. Any other business? Tony?
Tony:	Yes, just to say I'll be away on leave from Friday week and back not long before the dinner so can I have everybody's departmental expenses on my desk by the beginning of next week?
Chair:	Thank you. Let's minute that. And Frances.
Frances:	Yes, I've noticed we have a problem with our new post service. They're collecting in the evening but don't post until the following day. So it means we're losing a day on everything we send out. Can we make sure we get an earlier collection time to get same-day despatch?
Chair:	Thank you, Frances. Amy, can you investigate the postal collection situation and report back at the next meeting? Is there any other business? No? Amy, if you can send me the minutes, I'll circulate them. Thanks a lot everyone. OK, finally, the date of the next meeting is July 6th at 10 a.m. Well, that's it for now. Thanks again everyone.

Track 35

See the sentences in 7A.

Track 36

Model conversation

You:	*Thank you for coming. Could someone take the minutes?*
Elena:	I'll do it.
You:	*Thanks, Elena. OK, so the first item is last month's sales figures. John, could you speak about that?*
John:	Well, we were slightly ahead of budget and took a good order from a big supermarket chain. Nothing else to report really.
You:	*Thanks, John. Let's minute that we're ahead of budget and that we took this good order from a big supermarket chain. Let's move on to the next item – the new IT director. Elena, could you report on that?*
Elena:	Well, it's proving very difficult. We've decided to use a specialist recruitment company to find someone.
You:	*Fine. When do you hope to have someone in place?*
Elena:	We hope to have someone in place by the end of next month.
You:	*Thanks, Elena. OK, can I suggest we have a special meeting about this. Is Monday morning at 10 OK?*
Elena:	Good idea.
John:	In my diary.
Tom:	OK.
You:	*Good. Finally, is there any other business? Let's go round the table.*

Track 37

Chair:	Right, let's make a start everyone. So, on to the agenda. The motorway widening contract. Karen?
Karen:	We've got a problem with the schedule, Patricia. The project is currently running 12 weeks behind schedule.
Nick:	What? Twelve weeks!

Chair:	Hold on, Nick. Let's establish the facts first. Karen, why the delay?
Karen:	Basically, it's paperwork. Our joint venture partners are insisting that nothing is done until all documentation is up to date, and they're behind with the paperwork so nothing is happening.
Nick:	How come you didn't advise us immediately we fell behind?
Karen:	To be quite frank, we didn't know. Our joint venture partners didn't tell us about it until this week.
Chair:	So, let me summarize. We thought the project was on schedule. Our partners fell behind on paperwork so they delayed the start of construction until they caught up. Why?
Karen:	They needed local authority permissions and these were late coming through.
Chair:	So what's the main problem here as you see it?
Karen:	The problem is we don't control the schedule. We depend on our partner's reports to us and we only got the report on the delay this week.
Nick:	But it's your job to know. What are you project manager for if you can't control the schedule? You know there are penalty clauses if we don't complete on time.
Chair:	I don't think that is a matter for this meeting, Nick. Rather than looking to blame, let's look for solutions. Karen, what have you said to them?
Karen:	We've asked them to ignore the paperwork but they said they can't move without it and it's taking more time than expected.
Chair:	OK. So what are our options? So let's go round the table and get suggestions. Any ideas?
Barry:	Could I make a suggestion?
Chair:	Sure, go ahead, Barry.
Barry:	Can you meet with the joint venture project manager? What's his name? Gilberto? What's he like?
Karen:	Nice man. Good at his job.
Barry:	So why not have a meeting with Gilberto? Promise him that if he gets on with completing the project, our legal team will support him on completing the paperwork with the local authorities. If the paperwork *is* the problem, that will mean he can get back to work.
Chair:	Karen, what do you think? Could it work?
Karen:	I'm happy to try.
Chair:	Good. Thanks for that suggestion, Barry. Karen, report back at the next meeting, please, but in the meantime keep me in touch with developments on a daily basis. Is that OK?
Karen:	Fine. Will do.
Chair:	Good. We won't minute this discussion. We'll just minute that Karen is looking at ways of reducing delays on the schedule. OK?
Nick:	But we still have the problem of delays until they report them to us. We only know about them if and when they tell us. We can't have that.
Chair:	I take your point, Nick. Karen, could you also talk to Gilberto and arrange a weekly project phone conference to review deadlines and look at possible delays?
Karen:	Fine.
Chair:	And keep me posted on what he says. Let's review this next week. Same time, same place?
Karen / Nick / Barry:	OK. Yes.
Chair:	OK, thank you very much.

Track 38

See the sentences in 7B.

Track 39

Model conversation

You: *Right. Is there any other business? Let's go round the table. Elena, you first.*

Elena: Just one point. I'd like to raise the question of information transfer. No one told me about this meeting. I only found out about it on the general staff intranet this morning. I think that's unsatisfactory. Tom, you're responsible for communications and, frankly, you didn't communicate.

You: *Hold on, Elena. Tom, what's the problem as you see it?*

Tom: We're trying to save time and we're trying to reduce email traffic. So we decided to put the information on the intranet.

You: *Thanks, Tom. We need to make the information flow more effective. Any suggestions?*

John: Could I make a suggestion? It's fine to put meetings information on the intranet but you need to tell us as well.

You: *Good point, John. Any other suggestions?*

Elena: Yes, I can't always access the staff intranet when I'm out of the office. It's important to send me a meetings request to make sure I get it.

You: *Thanks, Elena. Tom could you send an email to all staff saying that you will post information about meetings on the intranet? Also, could you remind key personnel by sending a meetings request?*

Tom: OK. I'll do that.

You: *Thanks, Tom. Please keep me informed on developments and could you report back on progress at the next meeting? OK. AOB. Any other business? No? OK, let's agree the date and time of the next meeting. Next Thursday, same time, same place. OK. That's it. Thank you very much for coming.*

Unit 8   Participating in meetings

Track 40

Extract 1

Chair: Don, would you like to come in here? You wanted to say something about the implementation period, I believe.

Don: Yes, I did. Thanks. The key thing is how we manage this changeover. What I think we need to do is make sure that all departments …

Silvia: I don't think the main challenge is implementation …

Don: Silvia, please can I just finish what I was going to say?

Silvia: Sorry, I didn't mean to be rude. Please go on.

Don: That's OK. What I was going to say is this. We need to make sure that all departments understand the key deadlines for implementation. We all have to …

Extract 2

Don: John, could I come in here?

Chair: Yes, of course. What did you want to say?

Don: Thanks. I just wanted to say something about technical support during the implementation phase. We need to appoint technical experts who will support their colleagues.

Silvia: I'm afraid I don't think that will work.

Don: Why not? Why won't it work?

Silvia: Because they have their own jobs to do. We can't give them extra responsibilities during this implementation period.

Don: OK. Well, how about if we reduced their normal responsibilities during this period?

Silvia: That might work but it will need to be managed well.

Don: My main point is we need champions for the changeover. That's all I wanted to say.

Chair: Thanks, Don.

Track 41

See the sentences in 8A.

Track 42

Model conversation

You: *Could I come in here?*

Chair: Yes, of course. What did you want to say?

You: *Thanks. I just wanted to say something about budgeting for air travel.*

Sarah: But we've already discussed that!

You: *Hold on, Sarah. What I wanted to say is people can video-conference rather than have face-to-face meetings.*

Chair: That's a good point.

You: *My main point is air travel costs must come down.*

Chair: I agree with you.

You: *That's all I wanted to say.*

Track 43

Extract 1

Chair: Shall we turn to point 3 on the agenda, the appointment of a specialist business management system manager. Silvia?

Silvia: Well, what I wanted to say was that I don't think we have any good candidates in the company. What do you think, Don?

Don: I quite agree with you. There aren't any obvious candidates.

Chair: So what do think we should do?

Don: Well, I don't think straightforward advertising will work. I think we'll need to use an agency to find the right person.

Chair: You mean use a headhunting agency?

Don: Yes. We should advertise as well but we can't depend on that for success.

Chair: Silvia, what's your view?

Silvia: Well, I agree with Don up to a point. I just feel there's no point in spending a lot of money on advertising.

Don: I take your point. Maybe we should just advertise on our website. That costs virtually nothing.

Extract 2

Chair: OK, now we need to discuss the rollout period. We've talked about three months. Is that feasible?

Silvia: Definitely not. We need four months to implement the system across the whole company, at least four months, maybe longer.

Chair: And Don, your views? You look as if you want to say something.

Don: Well, with all due respect to Silvia, I completely disagree. I think we have to implement the new system very fast to get the momentum we need. I think three months is too long, in fact.

Silvia: Let's just examine the facts, Don. At present we have different systems for payroll, ordering and stock management, invoicing and payment, and so on, on 12 different sites around the world. This is a massive task.

Don: I agree you have a point there but …

Chair: What's the best way to resolve this?

Don: Well, I think we should draft a detailed plan for the rollout and see where that takes us.

Silvia: Absolutely! We definitely need more information to work with.

Track 44

See the sentences in 8B.

Track 45

Model conversation

Jenny: Can we all agree on the German management system?

You: *I have no objection to the quality but I have a strong objection to the price. It's too expensive. Can you find a cheaper option?*

Jenny: No, quality comes at a price.

You: *I agree up to a point but there are equally good local options, and they're cheaper.*

Jenny: Is there a cheaper option with the same quality?

You: *If we look at the situation objectively, the facts of the matter are these. We need excellent quality, good service, and a good price. Have you negotiated the best price?*

Jenny: Yes, I have. I don't know why you're objecting.

You: *Can I suggest a compromise? Get quotes from three suppliers, including local as well as foreign ones and let's see which is best.*

Jenny: I'm sorry, I think that's a waste of time.

You: *Well, I'm afraid we'll have to agree to differ on this one.*

Unit 9   Conference calls

Track 46

Chair: OK, let's start. Presumably everyone is here. Good morning, everybody. Let's update each other on progress on our different projects. Let's go round the table. Can I ask you, please identify yourself when you intervene and also make sure you speak clearly and concisely so we can all understand. OK? Bill, you first.

Bill: Thanks, this is Bill speaking. As you know, we're involved in a joint venture with Brazil to supply offshore cables for wind farms. We're in the middle of researching providers who can supply the right quality materials. We expect to get a result and make recommendations to the board of management and the client in the next two weeks.

Chair: Thank you, Bill, I think I got that. Keep me in the loop on that, please.

Jess: Jess, speaking. Bill, we have a list of suppliers of cable equipment including people we don't want to use. Would that be helpful?

Bill: Bill, speaking. Yes, it would. Thanks, Jess.

Chair: I think it would be good, Jess, to copy that list internally to all the people in the supply chain management process. Could you do that?

Jess: Jess speaking. Sure, as long as you remember it's for internal use only.

Chair: No problem, Jess. Thanks a lot. Now let's go on to Nina. [*silence on line*]

Chair: Nina, are you there? Nina?

Nina: Nina.

Computer-generated voice: … has joined the call.

Chair: Ah, finally. Welcome, Nina. Can you update us on progress on your project?

Nina: Good morning, everybody. Yes, well, as you know the project is about supplying an IT solution to our clients in Guangzhou in China. We've had meetings with them both here and on site and we've agreed the specifications and dimensions of the project and we now need to work on procurement and delivery of the solution. We're interviewing possible suppliers in five locations to decide on who is the most appropriate provider and will be able to make recommendations to the client at the end of the week.

Bill: I'm sorry, Nina. I didn't understand a lot of that. Could you summarize it for me, please?

Chair: Who's that? I can't hear anything. Please either press your mute button or get off the line. OK, that's better. Now, Nina?

Nina: Thanks. Let me just summarize. The client is in China. We're supplying IT solutions. We've agreed the specifications. We're interviewing suppliers.

Chair: Thank you, Nina. And when will that process be complete?

Nina: Hopefully by the end of the week.

Jess: I think we need a contingency plan in case things go wrong. There may be delays in procurement.

Bill: I'm sorry. Who's speaking now? Please identify yourself.

Jess: Sorry, it's Jess.

Track 47

See the sentences in 9A.

Track 48

Model conversation

Chair: Have you joined the call?

You: *Hi, everybody. I'm Harry Bailey from the US office in New York. I'm Supply Chain Manager.*

Chair: Hi, glad you could join us. Tell us what you're working on right now.

You: *Well, my current project is steel construction in Abu Dhabi. We're building a new terminal in the airport. So far we've designed the building and got the authorities' figures on price and specification and we're just about to interview providers for different components and services. We hope to begin construction in October and to complete the terminal within a year.*

Chair: Great. Thank you. Let me open up to questions. No? OK. Thanks very much.

Track 49

Model conversation

You: *OK, well, time is almost up. Let me summarize the key points but first, are there any questions?*

Harry: Yes, is there a central contact point we can use if we need to get in touch?

You: *Yes, I'll be the central contact point, at least for the time being, and I'll circulate my contact details at the end of this call. Any other questions?*

Harry: No.

You: *Fine, so to sum up, things are going well. First of all, Bill is waiting for recommendations about providers on the Brazil project and expects to have those in two weeks. Secondly, Jess will circulate a list of non-recommended providers, for internal use only. Nina is interviewing suppliers for the Guangzhou project and, finally, Harry is contacting potential suppliers for the Abu Dhabi airport terminal project. Have I missed anything?*

Harry: No, I don't think so.

You: *Great, so it's all systems go. Let's meet online again next week. I'll circulate possible dates and times. That's it. Thanks a lot and bye for now.*

Track 50

Chair:	Hi, Jess. Hi, Bill. Just to check, can you see Nina and me OK?
Jess:	Fine. No problem.
Bill:	Yes, fine.
Chair:	And how about sound? Is that all right?
Bill:	The sound's a bit distorted. Maybe we have a bad line. No, it's cleared up. Sound's OK now. We can hear you clearly.
Chair:	Good, let's get down to business. Nina and I just wanted to go through the SLAs first of all.
Bill:	Sorry? The …
Nina:	The SLA's – the service level agreements.
Bill:	Oh, right! OK. Sorry, I couldn't hear very well.
Chair:	[*pause*] Bill? Jess? Are you there? I can't see you!
Nina:	I think the satellite connection is down.
Chair:	Should we call a technician?
Nina:	I'm not sure. Let's just see if the picture comes back.
Chair:	No, it's OK now. The picture's come back. I can see you both again now. So, where were we?
Nina:	We were talking about the SLAs.
Chair:	Oh, yes. So Bill and Jess, can you tell us what you think …

Track 51

See the sentences in 9B.

Track 52

Model conversation

Customer:	As you know, in clinical trials, quality standards of health and safety and careful recording of samples and results are absolutely vital to the success of the trial. Can you reassure us on those points?
You:	*I'm sorry, I can't hear you very well. The sound is distorted. Could you repeat what you said?*
Customer:	I said, can you reassure us about your quality standards of health and safety?
You:	*I'm sorry, I can't see you or hear you clearly. Can you check the connection at your end?*
Customer:	[*pause*] Yes, our technical adviser has just checked the system and he says the satellite reception is fine again now. Can you hear and see me now?
You:	*Thank you. Yes, that's much better now. I can see and hear you with no problem.*
Customer:	As I was saying, can you reassure us about quality standards in clinical trials?
You:	*Yes. Every distributor and every operator in clinical tests has two weeks' health and safety training to international standards. [pause] I'm sorry, I can hear you fine but now I can't see you. Is the satellite down?*
Customer:	We're obviously having problems with reception at our end. Thanks for your answer. It may be best to continue the conversation by email.
You:	*It's OK. The satellite has come back up and reception seems to be OK now.*
Customer:	I think to save time it's better if we continue by email. Anyway, thanks for the reassurance on quality standards. Nice talking to you. Bye.

Unit 10 International negotiations

Track 53

Negotiator 1

First of all, before we get down to the negotiations, let me tell you a little bit about our company by way of an introduction. We're a food-processing company and I'm the European Sales Director. We're a family business and, in fact, the company was founded by my grandfather in the 1950s. We specialize in meat products, mainly chicken and beef. We have seven processing plants around Europe and we operate mainly in EMEA – that's Europe, the Middle East and Africa – and we supply own-brand products and other branded products to the leading supermarket chains. So that's us. Can you tell us a little bit about your company before we begin?

Negotiator 2

To start, let me tell you a bit about the company. We're an engineering manufacturing business and our key business is supplying components to companies that build and install wind farms. So it's quite specialist. And we're the second largest energy company in our sector. We were founded 30 years ago as an oil and gas company, specializing in offshore drilling components, but we moved into wind farm technology about ten years ago. Last year we turned over 150 million dollars and this year we're looking to increase revenues by 15 per cent. We have two manufacturing facilities, one in the UK and one in Korea.

Track 54

See the sentences in 10A.

Track 55

Extract 1

I think we can agree to those terms. We need to get our lawyers to draw up a contract and then go over the details. Let's proceed along those lines. Excellent.

Extract 2

So if we covered the costs of setting up the office in your building, you would be willing to give us the space rent free for the first 12 months?

Extract 3

So what you're saying is that you think you can help us in the US and Canada but that we might be better placed finding another partner for Mexico. Am I right in thinking this? Is this what you're saying?

Extract 4

I'm suggesting that we share the equity in the joint venture 60:40 in our favour. The reason for this is we have to keep ownership and control of our core products.

Extract 5

First of all, let me outline in general terms our needs. Our situation is that we're looking for a partner who can help us expand into the North American market with our products.

Track 56

See the sentences in 10B.

Unit 11 Negotiation styles

Track 57

Donna:	So, let's kick off. Let's agree the agenda first.
Nick:	Good idea.

Donna:	What are the key points for you?
Nick:	Well, product specification, price and delivery. Oh, and, of course, next steps.
Donna:	That's fine with me. And how do you want to proceed?
Nick:	I think the best procedure is for us both to state our positions, discuss and see what we agree on. What do you think about that?
Donna:	I'm happy with that. Shall I start?
Nick:	Go ahead.
Donna:	So, first of all, product specification. We see ourselves as a provider that does not compromise on quality. But quality comes at a price.
Nick:	So, could you say a bit more about that?
Donna:	Yes, of course. Do you feel your customers will pay higher prices for top quality product or do they want a range of products at different prices?
Nick:	What we'd like to achieve is a win–win situation for our customers, top quality at top price for those who can afford them but a range of prices for customers who want cheaper options. My question is: can you provide that?
Donna:	As I said, top quality product and service comes at a cost.
Nick:	So, what you're saying is this: you can provide us with top quality product and service but it will be at a premium price. We still need to discuss that price and the delivery system.
Donna:	Well, shall we move on to price?
Nick:	Yes, please go on.

Track 58

See the sentences in 11A.

Track 59

Model conversation

You:	*Thank you for coming. Let's kick off, shall we? Shall we start by agreeing the agenda?*
Negotiator:	That's fine with me. Those are the points I wanted to cover.
You:	*Fine. What procedure would you like to follow?*
Negotiator:	Well, if it's OK with you, let's both state our positions and then we can start to discuss them.
You:	*OK. Would you like to start?*
Negotiator:	Well, as I see it, the main issue we need to address is price. We need a range of cheaper products.
You:	*If I understand you correctly, you want us to expand our catalogue and offer cheaper products. Is that right?*
Negotiator:	Basically, yes. I think it will create a far more attractive sales proposition for you.
You:	*Mmm. Our organization has built up its reputation by word of mouth. This is because we have a reputation for high quality and our customers are prepared to pay a premium price for it.*
Negotiator:	So what you're saying is high quality, high price is good.
You:	*Yes, that's right. The market for luxury products is still expanding and we don't see a need to change strategy at this point.*
Negotiator:	And you don't think the situation will change?
You:	*That's not what I meant. If the market changes, we might consider new product ranges and a different pricing strategy. But we won't do that yet.*
Negotiator:	OK. So let's move on to point two on the agenda.

Track 60

Caroline:	So, let me make a proposal. Would you be prepared to make a trial order? It would be a good way to test the market.
Pete:	In principle we could consider that. But it would depend on price and on the possibility of sale or return.
Caroline:	We could offer you 1,000 units at list price but we'd be prepared to offer them on sale or return. How do you respond to this?
Pete:	Let me make another proposal. We will take 500 units as a trial order but we will feature it as a star buy on our website at premium price. We would pay list price on a sale or return basis.
Caroline:	What would you say if we offered you a 25 per cent discount if you took 1,000 units?
Pete:	Yes, we could do that as an introductory offer.
Caroline:	OK. Good. So you'll take 1,000 units at 25 per cent discount on our normal price. Now, do we have any flexibility on delivery?
Pete:	No, none at all. If we want to provide excellent customer service, the customer must know the delivery time the moment he or she signs on the dotted line. Delivery on demand is a key promise of our service.
Caroline:	We don't expect any problems but, if there is a problem, we offer a no-questions-asked refund.
Pete:	I'm afraid that's not good enough. Delivery is a key part of our service. We must respect that. If you can't deliver, then we must have a help desk with a real person answering the phone to help with any problems.
Caroline:	OK, we have a dedicated helpline and we can provide that service. Now, what about payment?
Pete:	All our contracts are signed on one basis, 90 days' payment. We would expect to do that with you.
Caroline:	Let me make a counter-proposal: we prefer to work on 60 days.
Pete:	I'm sorry. All our contracts work on 90 days and we pay on time. I'm afraid that is non-negotiable.

Track 61

See the sentences in 11B.

Track 62

Model conversation

You:	*Let's summarize what we've agreed so far. You agree to buy 1,000 units at 15 per cent discount but you require immediate delivery and you've asked for 90 days' payment terms.*
Negotiator:	That's right.
You:	*We've offered a no-questions-asked refund policy if there's any delay in delivery but you've said we must have a customer helpline in case of questions.*
Negotiator:	That's right.
You:	*The helpline is a development cost for us. Normally, we pass development costs on to the client. If we agree to pay the development cost, will you agree to 30 days' payment terms?*
Negotiator:	This is difficult for us. These are our standard terms and conditions.
You:	*Yes, but we're incurring extra costs and we need to recover our costs as soon as we can. If I suggested 60 days, would that be acceptable?*
Negotiator:	We've already agreed to take 1,000 units at 15 per cent. If we agree to 60 days' payment terms, will you agree to 20 per cent discount?
You:	*What if we split the difference at 17.5 per cent discount?*
Negotiator:	I suppose that's possible. OK.
You:	*Let me summarize what we've agreed so far: 1,000 units at 17.5 per cent discount, 60 days' payment terms, and we will organize a customer helpline for any customer problems regarding delivery.*
Negotiator:	I'll need to check my figures with our finance department but I think we can proceed along these lines.

Track 63

Karl:	Shall we check what we've agreed?
Annie:	OK. So we've agreed to create for you a specially adapted version of the product that you can sell to your clients under your own name.
Karl:	That's correct.
Annie:	We've agreed on price and delivery. The outstanding issue we face is how to pay for the adaptation. This is a development cost that we normally pass on to the client.
Karl:	I'm sorry, I can't agree to that. We're introducing your product to a new market at a premium price and we're asking for some small changes to make the product more saleable in our market, such as translation of the documentation, minor changes to the specification and rebranding. We don't expect to pay for that.
Annie:	But if we agree to pay for the change in branding and you pay for the translation and changes to the specification, will that be acceptable?
Karl:	Absolutely not, I'm afraid. The branding is a low-cost item. You're simply taking off your brand and putting on ours. Translation and changing the specification will cost more.
Annie:	OK. Suppose we agree to split the difference? Share costs on translation, adaptation and branding?
Karl:	My board won't like it. They expect you to pay for any development costs to adapt the product.
Annie:	Right. Well, as I see it, we have two alternatives. We can sell you the existing product with our brand on it or we can rebrand and adapt it and do the translation for you, and share costs. The problem with the first solution is that it will mean a much smaller market.
Karl:	Let me make another suggestion. Give us the existing version as it is. We will do the translation and brand it for our market. We will absorb the cost as an internal overhead and we will give you final approval on product quality. That way we can control costs and you still have quality control. I think I can sell that to my board.
Annie:	What about changes to the specification?
Karl:	We'll launch the version of the product without those and see how things go. We can come back and do that if it's a success.
Annie:	That might work. Let's take a break and think about it, and then discuss it in more detail when we get back to the table.
	[*pause*]
Annie:	Good news. I've talked to my board and they've approved your proposal. So I think we can proceed along the lines you suggested.
Karl:	Just so we're clear: you will give us the existing product. We will do the translation and branding for our market and you will have final quality control. Does that cover it?
Annie:	Pretty much. I think we have a deal.

Track 64

See the sentences in 12A.

Track 65

Model conversation

Negotiator:	OK, so we've agreed on specification, price and quantity.
You:	*That's correct.*

Negotiator: There's just the issue of delivery dates.

You: *Could you just explain what you mean?*

Negotiator: Well, we haven't fixed dates yet.

You: *Oh, you're right. How about the end of March for delivery of the units?*

Negotiator: I don't think we can manage that.

You: *An alternative might be half in mid-March and half in mid-April.*

Negotiator: That might be possible. I'll have to ask my board.

You: *All we need to do now is agree on this.*

Negotiator: I agree. We're nearly there.

Track 66

First phone call

Bob: Bob Smithies.

Gina: Hi Bob, it's Gina here.

Bob: Hi, Gina. How can I help?

Gina: I'm calling because I'm afraid we have a problem.

Bob: What kind of a problem is there?

Gina: As you know, we're currently going through the due diligence process and we've uncovered a discrepancy in your accounts.

Bob: What kind of discrepancy is that? You have our audited accounts. There shouldn't be any irregularities.

Gina: As I think you know, our offer to purchase your company was based on the understanding that there were no current debts. However, our due diligence on your accounts shows that you are still paying interest on a $500,000 bank loan you obtained two years ago.

Bob: Ah, I thought you knew that.

Gina: Well, we didn't.

Bob: We've agreed scheduled payments over the next year and a half and then we're in the clear. Our auditors have given us a clean balance sheet and our P&L is healthy. What will happen if we can't sort this problem out?

Gina: If we can't sort this out, then we may have to call off the deal. If we buy the company, we become responsible for the remaining loan repayments and we're not prepared to do that.

Bob: So how can we resolve the situation?

Gina: As I see it, we have two alternatives. Reduce our offer for your company or you pay off the outstanding loan and interest now so the deal can go ahead as planned.

Bob: And if I do that, can the sale go ahead?

Gina: Providing due diligence doesn't uncover any other problems, I don't see why not. I'm sure we can work this out.

Bob: Right. Can you give me a couple of days to consider my options? I'll come back to you as soon as I've talked to my finance people.

Gina: No problem. I just wanted to give you advance notice of the problem to give you time to find a solution. Can you come back to me with proposals by the end of the week?

Bob: I'll do that. Goodbye, Gina. And thank you.

Gina: No problem. We'll be in touch.

Second phone call

Bob: Gina. Hi, it's Bob. I said I'd get back to you on the accounts problem.

Gina: Thanks, Bob. And what do you propose?

Bob: I'm arranging a personal bridging loan with my bank to cover the interest payments on the loan and the outstanding capital but they want to know when I'll be able to repay it.

Gina: And ...?

Bob: Well, in order to do that I need to know how soon after contract I'll receive the purchase price for the company.

Gina: Well, in principle, provided that there are no more problems with due diligence, we would pay on signature of contract.

Bob: OK, I'll deal with it then. So the purchase price can remain as is.

Gina: Thanks, Bob. We appreciate that. Could you send me an email to confirm that and also a copy of the new loan agreement for our records?

Bob: Yes, I'll do that.

Gina: Thanks, Bob. I appreciate your cooperation and we'll be in touch very soon.

Track 67

See the sentences in 12B.

Track 68

Model conversation

Negotiator: Hi there. I'm calling because we have a problem.

You: *What kind of problem is there?*

Negotiator: We're preparing the contract now and I think we're making really good progress but we have a problem on exclusivity. Let me explain. We want world rights but we don't have rights to the US.

You: *Yes, we agreed to give you rights to the rest of the world but we want to keep the US rights.*

Negotiator: Our problem is that the US is our biggest market. We need US rights to deliver the revenues to meet the contractual payments to you. This is a deal-breaker for us. If we can't agree on this, we may have to withdraw from the agreement.

You: *This is a big deal for both of us. We're looking for a win–win agreement that will benefit both of us. Is it possible to meet halfway?*

Negotiator: Possibly. I think it's important we reach an agreement. What do you propose?

You: *How about this? We license US rights to you under a separate agreement provided you guarantee a higher proportion of revenue from US sales.*

Negotiator: Let me be sure I understand correctly. You will give us rest of world rights as agreed and you will give us US exclusivity under a separate agreement but you want a higher proportion of the US revenue. Is that right?

You: *That's right. I think this will help resolve the problem.*

Negotiator: OK. That's a positive proposal. I'll put it to the board. Thanks for your cooperation on this. I appreciate it. I'll get back to you as soon as possible.